THE BOOK OF
ST AUSTELL

THE BOOK OF
ST AUSTELL
A Celebration of a Cornish Town

PETER HANCOCK

HALSGROVE

First published in Great Britain in 2005

British Library Cataloguing-in-Publication Data.
A CIP record for this title is available from the British Library.

ISBN 1 84114 404 5

HALSGROVE

Halsgrove House
Lower Moor Way
Tiverton, Devon EX16 6SS
Tel: 01884 243242
Fax: 01884 243325
E-mail: sales@halsgrove.com
Website: www.halsgrove.com

Printed and bound in Great Britain by CPI Bath.

Title page: *Fore Street, c.1820.*

CONTENTS

ACKNOWLEDGEMENTS

I wish to thank the following individuals as well as staff at the institutions for their help during the compilation of this book:

Mr E. Anstey; Mr T. Allen; Mr F. Authers; Mr S.N. Beswarick; Mr J. Blake; Mr I. Bowditch of Imerys Minerals Ltd; Mr and Mrs F. Brewer; Mrs M.J. Chantry; Mr P. Clemo; Cornwall Record Office, Truro; The County Reference and Information Library, Truro; The Courtney Library, Royal Institution of Cornwall, Truro; Mr A. Deller; Mr J. Dove; Mr K. Dunstan; Mr R. Dutch; Mr T.A. Dyer; Mr S. Edyvean; Mr and Mrs L. Ford; Mr and Mrs W.A. Frazier; Mrs G. Gribble; Dr J.T. Hancock; Mrs Hazel Harradence of the Silvanus Trevail Society; Mr E. Jamilly, DipArch RIBA AC Arch; Mr L. Lean; Mr R. Metters; Mevagissey Museum; Mr W. Pappin; Mr R. Poad; Mr O.G. Richards; Mr S. Ridge; Messrs D. Rowe and B. Foster at the Eden Project; St Austell Library; Mr and Mrs R. Sandercock; The Shipwreck and Heritage Centre, Charlestown; Mr J. Stephens; Mrs M. Stephens; Mr D. Stone; Mr M. Stone; Mrs B. Webber; Mr T. Whetter; Mrs J. Wilcocks, Mr B. Yeo.

My grateful thanks are also extended to Naomi Cudmore, Katy Charge, Simon Butler, and all the staff at Halsgrove.

An early-nineteenth-century view of St Austell.

INTRODUCTION

The history of a town is also the history of its people. Yet St Austell is a place where the citizens who helped to mould it and who made it what it is today tend not to be commemorated personally, but are remembered because of the structures, big or small, that they left behind. Who was St Austell? Indeed, did a person by that name ever exist? The site of the cottage at Tregonissey where Dr A.L. Rowse spent his childhood is marked by a small and almost illegible plaque on the wall. Silvanus Trevail, the local architect responsible for some of the town's more noteworthy buildings, lies almost forgotten in Luxulyan churchyard, marked by a gravestone of his own design. Charles Rashleigh, founder of the port of Charlestown which bears his name, who resided in what was his town house, the White Hart Hotel, as well as Duporth House – unceremoniously destroyed in 1988 – and who had so much influence in the locality, is buried in an unmarked grave in the town's old cemetery. He shares his resting-place with many of St Austell's less illustrious and long-forgotten residents, whose graves are no longer even marked by their tombstones, now pushed up against the old wall like desultory ranks of exhausted soldiers. Many of them would have had such tales to tell of old St Austell and their lives spent there. What grief was felt at the funeral of Sarah Anne Anthony who died on 14 February 1826 aged one year and eight months – and again two years later when her brother John died aged one? What were the circumstances that brought Anna Marie Hatten of London to the town, only to die there on 3 February 1868, aged 20? And what of the people whose gravestones are broken or illegible?

There were the many unknown itinerant stone-masons who came to build the magnificent church tower back in the fifteenth century; the many unsung miners – men, women and children – who spent much of their pitifully short lives winning ore from the ground for the benefit of the landowners; the clay workers who excavated by hand the vast pits which scar the landscape. They all made a lasting mark on the area.

Similarly, many of the old names associated with the town's diverse businesses have gone and are being forgotten by successive generations. How many can recall Mr W. Avent who ran a bakery and confectionery business at Tregonissey; John Pooley's outfitters in Fore Street; Nancarrow's carpentry shop in Clifden Road; the boot repairer William Stone at Sandy Bottom; or stonemasons, Doney & Evans, who created many of those gravestones and monuments on their premises at Truro Road? It is hoped that this book will go some way towards redressing the balance.

Doney & Evans's fine premises still survive in Truro Road, although the stonemasons are long gone.

(Mr R. Poad)

The churchyard, c.1890.

Chapter 1

St Austell Through the Ages

There is plenty of evidence to suggest that the area has been occupied since prehistoric times: there is the Longstone, a standing stone now surrounded by the grounds of Penrice School; a barrow at Hensbarrow (another once existed on Gwallon Downs); while an ancient cliff-fort took advantage of the defensive position of Black Head. Bronze-Age and Iron-Age artefacts have been found. One of the most exciting pieces of evidence of our forebears was a hoard of silver treasure, buried at Trewhiddle in about AD875 and discovered in 1774. Yet what these ancient people called their home has not survived.

The Long Stone.

The Origins of the Name

The origins of the name St Austell seems to have been lost in the mists of time. Canon Hammond devoted a complete chapter to debating its origins in his book

Holy Trinity Church, c.1960.

A Cornish Parish without reaching a satisfactory conclusion. Austol may have been a missionary saint and a companion or acolyte of the missionary saint Mewan. Alternatively, he may not even have been a saint, but a hermit. There again, the name may not refer to a person but a building, such as a hostel or chapel connected with the priory at Tywardreath, to which the church owed allegiance for over 400 years.[1] It is stated in Pigot's *Directory of Devon and Cornwall* for 1830 that, 'The church is a fine old fabric, dedicated to Saint Austin'.[2] However, John Murray, in his *A Handbook for Travellers in Devon and Cornwall* states that the church is 'named, it is said, after St Auxilius'.[3]

The name St Austell does not appear in the Domesday Book of 1087. As a tax record William the Conqueror's survey was concerned with manors, hence the appearance of the local names 'Bewingtone' (Tewington), 'Treverbin' (Treverbyn) and 'Trenant' (Trenance). The name Trenance is preserved in the Trenance Valley. The closest recorded settlement in the Domesday Book is Trelowth.

The First Settlers

During the early Middle Ages the first settlers chose the site a little above the confluence of three valleys, Bodmin, Gover and Pentewan, not the most obvious place for a town to develop in Cornwall, being some distance from the coast or a navigable river. However, it was a good meeting point, blessed with fresh water from springs – such as St Austell Well and Menacuddle Baptistry – and with fertile land. The Mengu stone near the Parish Church, largely forgotten today, once marked the meeting point of the three manors of Tewington, Trenance and Treverbyn.

Written Records of the Town

The first written record of the town dates from 1169 and mentions Sancto Austolo. During the sixteenth century, Leland called it St Austelles, while Richard Carew in his *Survey of Cornwall* of 1602 refers to the town as *Trenas-austell*. However, within the next 50 years the current form of the name was adopted.

Over the years the town was described by a

Fore Street, early-twentieth century.

variety of travellers, not always in flattering terms. In 1824 the early travel writer Stockdale stated that, 'ST AUSTELL... is situated on the side of a hill, in a highly cultivated part of the county; it is now become a very populous market town'. He also noted that, 'the numerous Mines in the vicinity have raised it to an enviable rank of importance'.[4]

In 1859 Murray described St Austell thus: 'It is an old-fashioned and somewhat gloomy town, but can yet boast its cheerful villas on the outskirts'.[5] Pigot's *Directory of Devon and Cornwall* for 1830 noted that, 'The town derives its consequence and welfare from the mines in the neighbourhood, which are extensive and productive'.[6] This was still the case in 1873 when Kelly's *Directory of Cornwall* for that year described St Austell thus:

The town, situate [sic] on the southern slope of a hill, is of comparatively modern date, and owes its prosperous condition to the numerous tin and copper mines and china clay works in the surrounding district. The streets, though still narrow and irregular, have been much improved through the modernising of the old shops, and the erection of new buildings.[7]

W.H. Tregellas, writing in 1891, considered that the town 'contains in itself only one object of interest to the tourist – viz. the Church', although he went on to explain the best way of inspecting the 'clay-works' at Hensbarrow and Carclaze.[8]

The Carclaze Pit

During his visit in 1859, Murray was clearly very impressed with Carclaze Pit to the north of the town – by now becoming a celebrated tourist attraction – which he described as 'an immense tin-quarry' that could have been conjured up by a magician.[9] To reach it he suggested that the 'stranger' should head up the hill from the Mount Charles public house and look out for a cottage. 'This is the black-smith's shop at Carclaze, which is at the summit of a solitary moor commanding a fine prospect along the coast'.[10] He was in fact referring to the area known as Gwallon Downs, where there were clearly no other buildings at that time. Less than 150 years later the whole area had been built over, while somewhat ironically the surviving part of the blacksmith's shop – probably the one at Tregonissey Lane End and once run by the Mitchells – had also become a private residence.

Population of Town and Parish

Of the inhabitants themselves, Stockdale was able to say in 1824:

Although the manufactered [sic] commodities in St Austell are not deserving of mention, except it be in coarse woollens; yet its commerce in various branches is very considerable, and its inhabitants are in general remarked for being an industrious thriving people.[11]

Looking east across St Austell c.1910. The photograph was taken across open fields, from what is Edgcumbe Road in 2005. West Hill School, the Baptist chapel and the church are among the buildings easily identified on the right, and the workhouse is on the left. The words on the back are: 'A bird's eye view of St Austell. It is a very nice place. Very quiet.'

The town grew steadily during the nineteenth century. In 1801 the population of the town and parish amounted to just 3,788. In 1821 there were about 2,000 people living in the town, while the parish had 6,175 inhabitants. By 1831 this had risen to 8,758 and in 1841 to 10,320. By 1851 the population of the parish was 10,750, while the town itself housed approximately 4,000.

Water-Supplies

To sustain such a number of people, water was obtained from several sources. Canon Hammond stated that in 1786 water was brought from property owned by Mrs Mary Sawle of Penrice at Bojea. Later the town's water-supply was said to be dependant on

St Austell viewed from the east looking as if it was amidst a sylvan parkland setting. The postcard was published by 'J.W. & S., St Austell'.

'Lord Mt. Edgcumbe, whose tenants might at any moment, by their excavations, have cut it off at the source'.[12] No doubt to overcome this problem, in April 1896 a new water-supply was brought in 'amid considerable excitement'.[13] By 1923 a reservoir had been built at Trenance with a capacity of some one million gallons, supplied by a 'stream coming from Carn Stents and brought in by the Council at a cost of £5000'.[14] Of course, in 2005 the needs of the community are met by much larger regional reservoirs, and this most basic of requirements is taken for granted. Yet within living memory water had to be fetched from a communal tap; the alcoves that enclosed these, with granite pillars and lintels, still exist by the sides of many roads. Dr A.L. Rowse, writing in the early 1940s, recalls:

No one, I think, had water inside the house; the villagers fetched all their water from two public taps, which were, along with our shop, the chief news-centres and meeting-places the village [of Tregonissey] afforded.[15]

At that time a supply of fresh drinking-water was not guaranteed:

Sometimes water failed altogether and we took our pitchers to the clear-running stream which came out of the springs in the hillside and ran along in front of the houses at the other end of the village.[16]

Fortunately, water-supplies to the town were also maintained through periods of drought, for example,

11

The west end of Fore Street in the 1890s.

during the long, hot summer of 1976, and previously in August 1955:

> *Compared with the acute position in North Cornwall, the St Austell rural and urban areas are favourably placed. The prolonged drought has had a marked effect but only a few instances of a water shortage are reported by the two authorities.[17]*

Even as recently as 1950 the water-supply, then the remit of the local council, was one of their main items of expenditure. Interesting statistics were provided in the local newspaper for the area in that year:

> *St Austell Urban Council, administering an area of 18,379 acres with a population close to 24,000, spent £220,759 in the year 1949/50. A rate of 21s.2d. brought in £133,535 of this, and the rest was made up of grants, £35,666, rents, £26,983, and fees, £24,575.*
>
> *How was the money spent? Firstly, £82,270 went to the County Council for various services administered by that authority, such as education, roads, health, police, fire brigade, care of children and old people. The rest of the money, except for £157 spent on property valuation, went on services administered by the Urban Council itself, and of these housing, at £43,751, was by far the biggest.*
>
> *Other main items of expenditure were: water supplies, £17,817; highways and bridges, £17,398; refuse, £8,703; sewerage, £8,386; administration, £7,144; increased balances, £6,931; transport, £6,577;*

cemeteries, £3,765; parks, £3,478; health, £2,764; lighting, £2,474; beaches, £1,995; re-housing, £1,222; public offices, £1,213; public conveniences, £1,089; Mevagissey Town Hall, £305; emergency services, £103; other services, £3,217.[18]

It is easy to forget that many properties did not have running water or indoor sanitation until after the Second World War. If they were lucky, cottagers enjoyed the luxury of a brick privy at the bottom of the garden. Dr A.L. Rowse commented on this situation at Tregonissey:

> *I doubt if there was a single water-closet in the whole place. Most houses shared earth-closets, one to two or three houses; you can imagine to what quarrels that led with regard to respective rights and duties.[19]*

The situation in his own neighbourhood he recalled as follows:

> *Such drains as Tregonissey possessed were open drains: I am not sure that even the plural here is not a mistake. All your slops and dish-water you had to take across the road and empty into the open drain which ran along in front of our house, if on the opposite side of the road – a distinction which made little difference in hot, smelly summer weather.[20]*

He put the people's good health down to plenty of fresh air. The streams that emerged as springs in the

A quiet Penwinnick Road leading to the bypass, 1960s. One of the two gasometers can be seen on the left, removed during the late 1960s. (Mr R. Dutch)

hillside now flow unseen in the drains beneath the roads.

Electricity and Gas

Mevagissey was one of the first places to have electricity. There was a small power station on West Wharf beneath Polkirt Hill run by Mr Sidney. Local children used to enjoy looking through the doorway at the machinery which included a paraffin engine with a single fly-wheel used to power the generator. Initially it ran some lights strung from poles around the harbour. Mains electricity arrived in the village in the early 1930s; when the trenches were dug in Fore Street to lay the cables, golden sand could be seen at the bottom of them.

St Austell had two gasometers for storing coal gas. Like many towns the large grey cylindrical towers were a feature of the skyline until the 1960s.

St Austell Gas Co. Ltd suggested using coal gas for everything (from Harding's Guide Map to the District of St Austell, c.1920s).

Local Schools

St Austell won a claim to fame when the first Board School in England was built at Mount Charles in 1870. Soon other schools were built to serve the local community, such as Carclaze County Junior School in 1878. Later this became the Infants' School, and a new school building was constructed in the 1950s on open land to the south of Carclaze Road that had been the playing-field. Village schools were also built throughout the surrounding area. Older children were catered for by St Austell County School, dependant on winning scholarships or parental subsidies, or West Hill Secondary School, known as Central School because it also attended to the needs of the outlying districts.

Some private schools that once existed in the town have been consigned to history. The Ordnance Survey map of 1888–1889 clearly shows that a school once existed at Treleaven Cross, Polkyth, where the council-houses now stand. Weston House School, where the Revd Richard Sampson was principal, was also listed in Kelly's *Directory of Cornwall* of 1873. The advertisement in this volume boasted that during 'examinations in May, 1872, Nineteen 'Passes' and Eleven 'Prizes' were obtained', as well as stating that 'Each boarder has a separate bed'. The school had a 'staff of 5 resident & two visiting teachers (including a resident master – foreign – for French & German)'.[21] Terms were priced at 25 to 30 guineas, while in addition washing could be done at 5s. per quarter and chemistry was offered at 10s. per quarter.

Moorland House School in South Street appeared in the Kelly's 1923 *Directory of Cornwall*; at that time Miss L.M. Hawley was principal. It was advertised as a 'boarding & day school for girls & little boys', offering a 'thorough education on Modern Lines' comprising 'Games, Dancing, Drill for Moderate Fees, as well as a resident French Mistress'.[22] More successful perhaps was the Lawn School in Truro Road which gained an enviable reputation between

A class at the County School for Girls, segregated at the time. The boys' school was built in 1906 and the girls' in 1931. Together they continue as Poltair Community College. (Mr R. Dutch)

Council School, West Hill, St Austell, 1905.

Mount Charles Infants' School, 1927/28. Left to right, back row: Marion Daniel, Kathleen Jenkins, Rosie Pope, ?, Pearl Trethewey, Nancy Greenslade, Valerie Armstrong, ?, Molly Huddy, Doreen Cory; middle row: Bill Husband, Jack Rowett, Norman Taylor, ? Taylor, Kathleen Palmer, Betty Squires, Audrey Stone, Betty Ball, ? Rowe, Isabel Parsons, Ivy Matthews, Enid Trevan; front row: Leslie Martin, Eric Davey, Leslie Nile, Leonard Finch, Dennis Sandercock, Morley Webber, Owen Rowe, George Sidwell, Wilfred Rowe, ?, Geoffrey Phillips. (MRS B. WEBBER)

Mount Charles School, 1907. Mount Charles had the distinction of being the first Board School in England, following the 1870 Education Act. (MRS B. WEBBER)

A class of Mount Charles School, c. 1932. The Infant School was then a separate building.

Mount Charles School, 1937. (MRS B. WEBBER)

Carclaze County Junior School, 1934. Left to right, back row: *Roy Edwards, Gerald Ayres, Christine James, Doreen Lamerton, Joyce Varcoe, Mary ?, Phylis Werry, Harry Deal, Bobby Keat;* third row: *? Tucker, Doris Ruse, ?, Iris Dowrick, ?, ?, Megan Larcombe, Barbara Grose;* second row: *Roy Hocking, Norman Dawe, Colin Corin, Arthur Sandry, Dennis Yates, ?, Billy Martin, Harry Rowett, Ivor? Bassett;* front: *Sidney Adison, Les Ford, Gerald Lockett, Harold Hambly, Alfred Geach, ?, Donald O' Shea.* (MR & MRS L. FORD)

Carclaze County Junior School, 1935. The bottom of the picture stated that it was the silver jubilee for their Majesties, the King and Queen, i.e. George V and Queen Mary. Left to right, back row: ?, ?, Jim Mitchell, Harry Deal, David Gammon, Tom Menear, ?, Leslie Heaman, ?, ?; third row: Colin Corin, Bill Sweet, Horace Hancock, Roy Edwards, Gerald Ayres, Roy Rosewear, ?, Arnold ?, ?, ?, ?; second row: Bill Hender, ?, ?, ?, Kenneth James, ?, ?, ?, Les Ford; front row: Reginald Pope, ?, Donald O' Shea, ?, ?, ?, Harry Rowett, ? Nile. (Mr & Mrs L. Ford)

Jack and the Beanstalk *being performed by the children of Carclaze Infants' School, c.1968.*

Carclaze School, seen in splendid isolation, 1960s. In the foreground a bungalow is being set out in neighbouring Agar Road; some years later houses were built at Phernyssick.

(Mr R. Dutch)

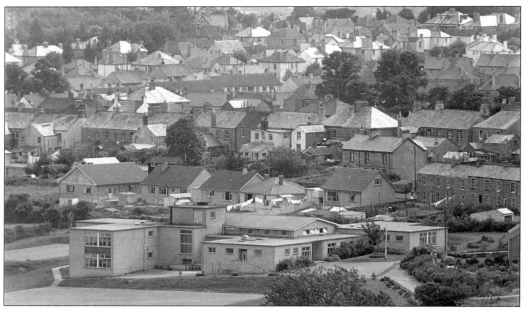

Carclaze School, new bungalows in Agar Road, and behind them, the back of houses lining Slades Road photographed during the early 1960s. The delightful mural of St Francis of Assisi that originally adorned the wall of the stairwell in the central portion of the school, and is remembered by many former pupils, no longer exists.

(Mr R. Dutch)

Whitemoor School, November 1936. The teacher is Mr Roberts.
(Mrs D. Billing)

A group photo of Whitemoor School, 1952/3. (Mrs D. Billing)

Members of St Austell Grammar School perform A Midsummer Night's Dream *in what was an ideal venue between the dining-hall and the main school building. The courtyard where the audience sat (including photographer Roy Dutch) was used for an extension in 1992.*
(Mr R. Dutch)

'Good Luck from St Austell', c.1930. The four views show Pentewan (the school can clearly be seen on the right, as well as the blockworks from where the sailing club operates in 2005); Porthpean with Mrs Hunkin's tea shop; Charlestown with Appletree Mine standing out on the promontory; and the Parish Church surrounded by palm trees.

1901 and the 1970s, while Roselyon at Par continues to thrive in 2005.

Meanwhile, to cope with the growing population, state schools have been built or have gained new buildings. For example, a modern school was built at Mount Charles and the old Victorian school building, designed by Silvanus Trevail, was turned into apartments. Likewise, Charlestown's original school, built in 1895, was replaced with a new building on much larger grounds at nearby Campdowns, while the original building, for a while used by Charlestown Joinery, has been converted into apartments. Biscovey gained a new school in 1966, and in 1979 Bishop Bronescombe School near Bethel was opened to cater for that growing area of the town, being named after the thirteenth-century bishop who originally dedicated Holy Trinity Church.

Population and Migration

By 2000 the population of St Austell itself had reached 19,710, making it the largest town in the county. In April 1974 the *Cornish Guardian* had predicted that:

A million and a quarter more people than at present will be living in the seven counties of the South West by the end of the century – more than half of it as result of migration.[23]

It would prove to be a prophetic statement, with Cornwall, and St Austell in particular, being the focus of this migration. To sustain this increased population, large housing estates have been built, and continue to be, on any convenient brown-field site, as well as on open fields on the edges of the town.

The Borough of Restormel

The Borough of Restormel was created on 1 April 1974, under the provisions of the Local Government Act 1972, and was one of six districts in the county. Newquay Urban, St Austell with Fowey Borough and St Austell Rural Councils were combined to make up Restormel (at the same time as the controversial Rate Support Order against which many protested). In 2005, Restormel's population is 97,880; it is the most heavily populated of the county's six districts and covers an area of 180 square miles.

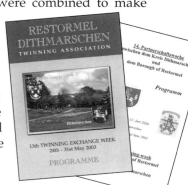

Two programmes produced by the Restormel/ Dithmarschen Twinning Association in June 2003 and 2004, outlining the wide range of events laid on during the twinning weeks.

Fore Street during the 1950s was a vibrant main street. Before pedestrianisation, this MG TD was free to use the thoroughfare. (MR R. DUTCH)

The Twinning of Restormel and Dithmarschen

In 1990 Restormel was formally twinned with Dithmarschen in Germany – and the drive leading into the new council offices at Pondhu was christened in honour of Dithmarschen. An exploratory visit had taken place in November 1989 during which the Mayor of Restormel, George Down, was accompanied by Jozsef Varga (councillor), David Brown (chief executive) and 'Ebby' Anstey (director of tourism).

Dithmarschen is a district in Schleswig-Holstein in north-west Germany. It covers an area of 1,425sq km, much of it low-lying, as half of it has been reclaimed from the sea, creating fertile farmland – known as the *Marsch*. Dithmarschen is defined by the North Sea, River Eider, River Elbe and the Kiel Canal. It has a larger population than Restormel, comprising some 130,000 people. Social and cultural twinning events have taken place annually, the venue alternating each year between the two regions. These events were initially administered by the Borough Council, but in 2000 a Twinning Association was created, presided over by the Mayor of Restormel.

One of the principal aims of the twinning has been for families from each country to act as hosts for their counterparts, and where possible to match guests who have similar interests, such as golf, music or angling. Since the partnership began, over 100 different clubs and organisations have participated, ranging from women's institutes, artists and folk singers, golf and sailing clubs, to schools and colleges.

The Town Centre

The town itself has been less successful at keeping up with the demands placed upon it by this growing population. The high hopes engendered by the creation of the new town centre during the 1960s failed to materialise. As a shopping centre the town fell into decline towards the end of twentieth century, when it struggled to compete with growing out-of-town shopping centres and supermarkets, as well as from more forward-thinking rivals such as Truro. Since the millennium, plans to regenerate the town with another new town centre have been slow to materialise, leading some to now dub it 'St Awful'.

Despite this, in a survey of over 600 local residents conducted by Restormel Borough Council in 2002, 60 per cent replied that they were very satisfied with their neighbourhood as a place to live.[24]

References

[1] Joseph Hammond, *A Cornish Parish: Being an Account of St Austell, Town, Church, District and People*, p.8.
[2] Pigot's 1830 *Directory of Devon and Cornwall*, p.161.
[3] John Murray, *A Handbook for Travellers in Devon and Cornwall*, p.242.
[4] F.W.L. Stockdale, *Excursions in the County of Cornwall*, p.47.
[5] John Murray, *op. cit.*, p.242.
[6] Pigot's 1830 *Directory of Devon and Cornwall*, p.161.
[7] Kelly's 1873 *Directory of Cornwall*, p.705.
[8] Walter H. Tregellas, *Tourist Guide to Cornwall and the Scilly Isles*, p.72.
[9] John Murray, *op. cit.*, p.243.
[10] *Ibid.*
[11] F.W.L. Stockdale, *op. cit.*, p.48
[12] Joseph Hammond, *op. cit.*, footnote on p.35.
[13] *Ibid.*
[14] Kelly's 1923 *Directory of Cornwall*, p.24.
[15] A.L. Rowse, *A Cornish Childhood*, p.19.
[16] *Ibid.*
[17] *Cornish Guardian*, 18 August 1955, p.8.
[18] *Cornish Guardian*, 15 November 1950, p.5.
[19] A.L. Rowse, *op. cit.*, p.18.
[20] A.L. Rowse, *op. cit.*, p.20.
[21] Kelly's 1873 *Directory of Cornwall*, p.58. The examinations quoted were taken in the Science and Art Department at South Kensington.
[22] Kelly's 1923 *Directory of Cornwall*, p.5.
[23] *Cornish Guardian*, 25 April 1974, p.1.
[24] Restormel Borough Council, *Quality of Life Report – 2003*, p.4.

Chapter 2

A Historical Tour of the Town Centre

Opening Hours

Before the Second World War St Austell was a busy market town. Before cars were universally available people would arrive by bus from the outlying areas. From Mondays to Wednesdays most of the butchers, grocers and newsagents were open for business between 8a.m. and 6p.m. Tuesdays saw farmers arriving to attend the cattle market, often accompanied by their wives who would spend the day shopping. On Thursdays the shops opened from 8a.m. until 1p.m. due to half-day closing. Friday was market day, with shops open from 8a.m. to 7p.m., and Saturdays were always busy with most shops open from 9a.m. until 8p.m. On Saturday afternoons the streets, and in particular 'Fools' Corner' outside the church, were social venues where many youngsters would congregate for a chat. Sunday opening was unheard of, and anyway, being the Sabbath, most people attended church or chapel.

Courteous Service

Customers took notice of the window displays, comparing prices between shops before buying. For example, in Miss Pope's window, (described in Kelly's *Directory of Cornwall* as a 'fancy repository') there was an array of skeins of silk and wool. Courteous and obliging shop staff offered a personal counter service, and many shops would provide a chair for the elderly to sit on. Often commodities would be weighed up and wrapped as needed.

An early view of Tidy's Corner, the junction between Fore Street on the left, Truro Road on the right, and Bodmin Road. It is hard to imagine stables in Fore Street, or the poor state of the road. The Liberal Club would be built here by 1890. (MR R. DUTCH)

When orders were taken the grocery goods were delivered by an errand boy on a bicycle (see Chapter 7), butchers' meat by pony and trap, while the ironmongers used vans.

Goods and Prices

In 1930 2lb of granulated sugar cost 4½d.; New Zealand Anchor butter, 1s.3d; currants or sultanas, 6d. a pound; dried prunes, 4d.; a tin of pineapple cubes was 4½d. A 2lb jar of jam was 10½d., but shrewd customers could get ½d. back by returning empty jars. Other items, such as slab cake, cheese and bacon had to be weighed using balance scales and weights and priced accordingly. Then of course, the housewife might require a tin of Zebo at 7½d. to polish her black stove and fireplace.

Security

At the end of the day, money was rarely placed in a shop safe for the night. Instead, each day at about 2p.m., the takings were banked. The rest of the day's takings were placed in a bag at closing time and secreted amongst the packets of goods in the shop. Crime was rarely an issue – few people locked their doors. The town would have a policeman on the beat, urging small crowds to 'move along', or trying to sort out the chaos caused by two-way traffic in Fore Street, particularly when loaded clay wagons pulled by three horses passed through, en route for Charlestown. Today we might complain about litter, but that was nothing compared with spilt china clay and horse droppings.

Traffic and Congestion

Traffic congestion was at its worse during the summer months. In August 1929 it was reported in the *Cornish Guardian* that:

Clay wagons at Foundry Hill.

Fore Street in 1963, long before it was pedestrianised. (MR R. DUTCH)

An advertisement for Tom J. Smith who ran his business from 32 Fore Street as a cabinet-maker and upholsterer in 1894. No MDF or flat-packed furniture was available then! (MR R. POAD)

Grocer and flour merchant R.N. Rogers had premises at 28 Fore Street in 1894. (MR R. POAD)

Many times during the week motorists find themselves in a traffic block in Fore Street, with its attendant inconvenience, to say nothing of damaged mud-guards and scratched panels sustained through the necessity of backing to allow oncoming traffic to pass.[1]

One-way traffic was eventually introduced in the 1950s and Fore Street was pedestrianised during the 1980s. Soon the street was paved with ubiquitous paving-bricks, and decorated with cast-iron bollards and black steel planters modelled on clay skips. A pair of decorative gates was placed at the western end of Fore Street, effectively closing it off to traffic at various times.

Local Businesses

The type and variety of shops has changed dramatically over the years. At the end of the nineteenth-century cabinet-makers and upholsterers kept premises in Fore Street. Just off Fore Street, behind the New Inn in Chandos Place where coaching horses used to be left for the night, H. Jenkin, a farrier and general blacksmith, was to be found. The old yard of the inn, as well as a butcher's shop, was developed when Woolworth's was built. When the shop opened on 11 November 1927, it was not only the first

The Public Benefit Boot Company had premises in Fore Street in 1923. The manager is Henwood Sprague, standing in the doorway with his assistants. He was later transferred to Norwich. (Mrs I. Hancock)

Woolworth's in Cornwall, but deemed to be 'the most modern store of its kind'.[2]

Other businesses included C.F. Collins, a saddler and harness-maker in Duke Street, and F. Cox & Son, a cycle agents in both Fore Street and Duke Street. There were also dressmakers, cooks and confectioners, boot makers, ironmongers, as well as general grocers who operated as flour merchants and tea dealers.

No. 19 Fore Street was, during the 1930s, occupied by a number of china clay companies, such as Frederick Liddicoat, a china clay merchant; Melangoose China Clay Company; Newton Abbot Clay Ltd; as well as Paper Makers' Chemicals Ltd, who manufactured size (a gelatinous solution made in glazing paper), and Paper Makers' Importing Company. It would not be long before such private firms were absorbed into larger companies or disappeared entirely.

Today we would not consider visiting an ironmonger if we required a new bed or bedding but, in 1894, T. Mann's shop in Fore Street was the place to buy iron and brass bedsteads, as well as bedding. (Mr R. Poad)

George Hawke & Son (from Harding's Guide Map to the District of St Austell, *c.1920s).*

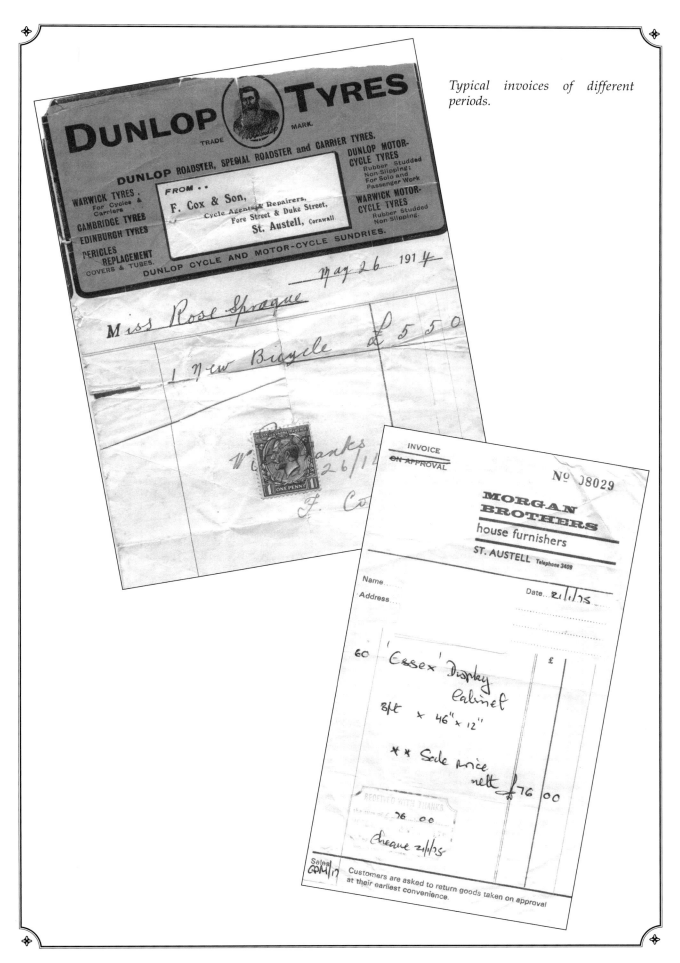

Typical invoices of different periods.

Name ....
Full address ..
....
....

Sale Invoice № 006615
FROM...
BROAD (St. Austell) Ltd.
27, FORE STREET,
ST. AUSTELL, PL25 5PT   Tel. 2345/6

| Date 30/12/19 74 | Entered by 16 | Passed by | Taken/Delivery |

Dept.	Quantity	Description	Price each	TOTAL
67	10 yd	VELVET. e	£3·10	£31·00
67	10 yd	LINING. e	70p	£7·00·
67	5½ yd	REGIS TAPE e	42p	£2·31
40	2	SYLKO e	10p	20
67	9 ft	SOLOGLIDE RAIL e	23p	£2·07
67	1	CORDING SET.		£1·18
98		To MAKE CURTAINS		£14·00
98		To FIX RAIL & CORDING SET. & HANG CURTAINS		£3·00
				£60·76

V.A.T. No. 131 6270 03

CARLYON BAY GARAGES LTD.

CARLYON BAY - ST. AUSTELL PL25 3PL
PAR (072 681) 4081
VAT Registration No. 131 6039 05

ROVER

Invoice To   Supply To   PARTS SALES INVOICE

Date/Tax Pt : 27/04/89
Document No : 000708
Sale Type   : RETAIL
Payment   : CASH
Order Number :
Raised By   : R
                  Page 1

P.V.C. Roof Sheets
Perspex
Plastic Foam

ADVICE / INVOICE

EVANS & SONS

Hardware
Ironmongery / D.I.Y.
Garden Tools
Camping

MARKET HOUSE, ST. AUSTELL, CORNWALL
Tel : ST. AUSTELL (0726) 3777

V.A.T. REG. NO. 131 9548 66

Mr. Hancock   21.5. 19.83

1	Suffolk Punch Motor 14 35DL	203	99
	less 20% Discount	40	79
Paid Cheque		163	20

Williams

№ 3880

Invoices from various local businesses.

There were a number of shops in Duke Street in 1894, including M. E. & L. Hurden, 'High Class Dressmakers'. (MR R. POAD)

George Hawke & Son stocked a wide range of goods, as shown in this advertisement from 1894. (MR R. POAD)

An advertisement from 1894 for two businesses in the town that no longer exist in 2005: W. Warne & Sons and W. Treganowan. (MR R. POAD)

W.B. Luke also had premises in Fore Street, in 1894. The business was not only a printer's and stationer's, but also sold musical instruments. (MR R. POAD)

Mr Ernest Hugo, c.1913. The photograph was taken by E.J. Russell, who held premises in Duke Street. (MR P. CLEMO)

In 1930 there were ten grocers' shops in St Austell, starting at Fore Street with Lipton's, Thomas's, Home and Colonial, Star Tea Company (later International), Co-operative, Percy Prout's, and Peark's Stores. Michael's Stores was in Cross Lane, Box's Stores in Church Street and Paul's Shop at the bottom of East Hill. Besides these there were four butchers' shops: Hoar's at West End; Fred Hart's in Fore Street; Eastman's next to Woolworth's and Stephens's at East Hill (Cooksley's in 2005). The town also boasted six drapers, three

Roy Dutch's 'Projector Week' (advertised in the Cornish Guardian, *21 August 1967, p.2).*

bakers, six men's outfitters, three jewellers, three ironmongers, three chemists, three newsagents, three china shops, one seedsman, two paint shops, and three sweet and tobacco shops.

Banks and Finance

During the period 1790–1840 it was common for towns in Britain to have their own banks, many of which were set up by wealthy merchants. Before they merged into the large international institutions that we see today, they were not always the most secure place to invest money. One such example was Philip Ball & Son, founded in Church Street, Mevagissey in 1807, who later established a branch in St Austell. They even issued their own £1 and £5 notes. However, when faced with an economic slump, Philip Ball, who had widespread local interests including farming, the china clay industry and St Austell Foundry, as well as the Charlestown and Mevagissey harbours, found that he could not settle with his creditors and was declared bankrupt in 1824. Clearly this brought a great deal of hardship to many.

Hodge's ironmonger's in August 1933. In the doorway are Mr Dennis George, Mr Jack Blake and Mr Charlie Hammer. On the right is a delivery bicycle of the neighbouring Boots the chemist. It is interesting to note the old lamps in the window, besides the galvanised bucket and coal scuttle suspended above the door. (Mr J. Blake)

Local Publications

The town also had a number of local newspapers. The weekly *St Austell Gazette* was published from 1870 until 1878. The *St Austell Star* appeared on 15 March 1889, printed by Sanders Brothers of Grant's

Timothy White's party, 1929, held in the Capitol Theatre.   (Mr J. Blake)

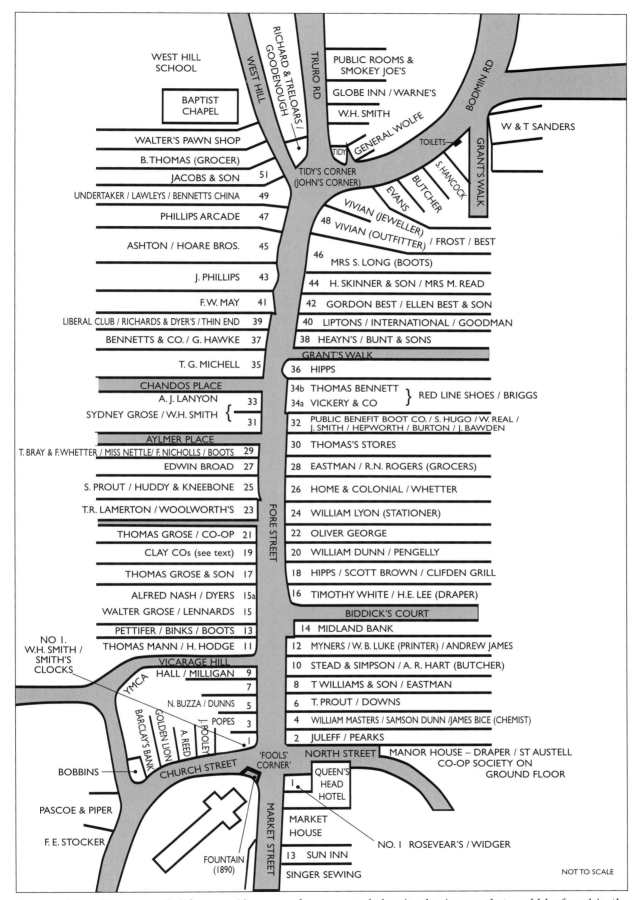

A map of Fore Street compiled from a wide range of sources, and showing businesses that could be found in the main street over a large number of years.

The fire in Fore Street which destroyed the Co-op store on 18 October 1940.   (Mr R. Sandercock)

Walk for the proprietor, Walter John Nichols of St Austell. Later the task of printing the *St Austell Star* was given to a Plymouth printer, so Sanders Brothers brought out their own *St Austell Gazette & Mid-Cornwall Advertiser*. After 97 issues had been printed the quarrel was settled and the *St Austell Star* and *St Austell Gazette* merged to become simply the *St Austell Star*. There was also the *St Austell Gazette & Cornwall County News* which ran from 10 March 1926 to 9 March 1951, and *St Austell Weekly News & County Advertiser* which began in July 1868, and was published by Philip Giles and later William B. Luke. The *Cornish Engine Reporter*, a monthly publication, appeared in February 1847 and was printed by Jacob Halls Drew of St Austell for the proprietor, William Browne of Charlestown. (The *Cornish Guardian*, an important source of news for local people today, was a relative latecomer, being first published in 1901 in Bodmin.)

A Fire in Fore Street

On 14 October 1940 the Co-op store in Fore Street caught fire, an event that is still remembered by many of the older generation in 2005. It is possible that the fire may have been started when an engine in the cellar backfired. Certainly the blaze was soon intense. Witnesses recall barrels in the nearby New Inn popping from the heat. Pedestrians were stopped from walking through the street as the local fire brigade fought to contain the fire and prevent it spreading to neighbouring shops such as Woolworth's. Buildings to the rear of the shop in

Fore Street in 1953. The derelict site on the right is the remains of the Co-op shop, gutted by fire in 1940.

(Mr R. Dutch)

Chandos Place were damaged. The burnt-out shell of the Co-op had to be demolished, and the site remained empty until new shops were built during the 1960s.

Improving the Town Centre

The creation of St Austell's new town centre was intended to enlarge and enhance the shopping area. The scheme was made public in April 1957 when it was stated that the 'shopping area could be nearly doubled'; it was, however, estimated that the completion of the scheme could take up to ten years.[3] This proved to be an accurate prediction.

A new link road was created in the form of Trinity Street, and a number of shops including Phillips Arcade, were demolished to make way for a new road junction. The new street caused a number of unforeseen problems for neighbouring West Hill School but, on the other hand, new shops, garages and flats were created, while a multi-storey car park was built for the convenience of shoppers. Behind Fore Street, utilising an area of waste ground and a maze of alley-ways and run-down buildings that extended as far as the Odeon cinema, Aylmer Square was built. Buildings that had once formed Burton Court, Aylmer House and Chandos Place were levelled and a new square created, bordered by shops with flats above. A new Vicarage Place would be added in 1984, making use of wasteland between Duke Street and the Odeon cinema.

East Hill

East Hill, one of the main turnpike roads leading into the town from the east, has changed dramatically over the years. Below Hilltop Terrace with its façade of decorative red and cream bricks was a hotchpotch of cottages at Paul's Square and Merrifields. This

W.H. Lake & Son (from Harding's Guide Map to the District of St Austell, *c.1920s).*

T. Treleaven's 'depot' (from Harding's Guide Map to the District of St Austell, *c.1920s).*

Sprague's coach builders was located at the bottom of East Hill, c.1910.

Destruction of old buildings at what would become the entrance to Trinity Street, 1961/2. The Baptist chapel at the top of West Hill would be spared and survives in 2005. There was no health warning on tobacco advertising back then; Craven 'A' cigarettes 'Will not affect your throat', but it didn't mention the smoker's lungs!

(MR R. DUTCH)

The new junction between Truro Road and an all new Trinity Street, that would be dubbed 'Roundabout' corner, 1966. (MR R. DUTCH)

Buildings under construction in Trinity Street during 1966, referred to on the plans as Blocks 'W' and 'F'. (MR R. DUTCH)

Block 'L' towards the bottom of Trinity Street still under construction in 1966. The notorious multi-storey car park can be seen on the right, in front of the Odeon cinema. The sign informs onlookers of the contractors, Selleck Nicholls Williams Ltd. (MR R. DUTCH)

According to the plans, Block 'A' of the new town centre would provide garages on the ground floor, then shops and showrooms, with flats above. (Mr R. Dutch)

A fleet of lorries pictured in 1944 in the old Odeon car park which now forms part of Trinity Street. The depot was in Moorland Road. The three vehicles on the left sported yellow crosses on their cabs as they were used at airfields, particularly here in the West Country. (Mr A. Deller)

The condemned old houses that were in Burton Court, photographed in c.1960. This maze of houses and alley-ways was once behind the west end of Fore Street. (Mr R. Dutch)

A shot of Aylmer Square during construction, taken from the Odeon cinema in 1966. Some shops are already being occupied, while others are still being fitted out.　　　　(Mr R. Dutch)

Another view of Aylmer Square in 1966, showing Blocks 'M' and 'E' still under construction. Many of the walls were built from 'Reformite', produced at Gothers by ECLP.　　(Mr R. Dutch)

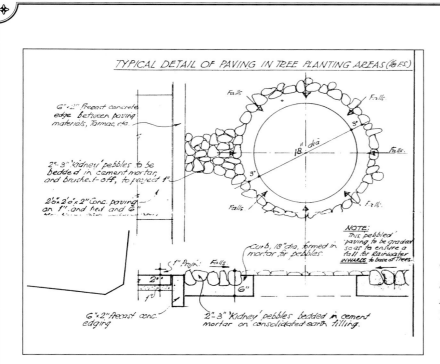

The precinct layout of Aylmer Square, produced by Alister Mac Donald & Partners in 1964.

(Mr E. Jamilly, DipArch RIBA AC Arch)

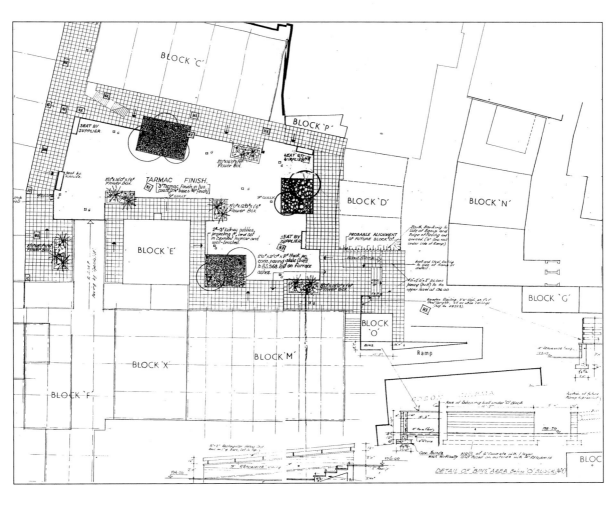

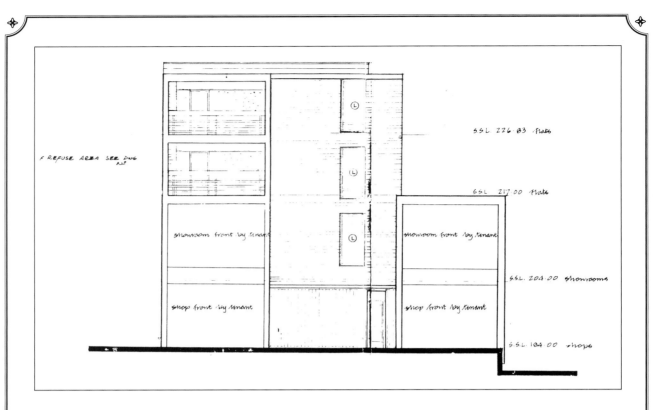

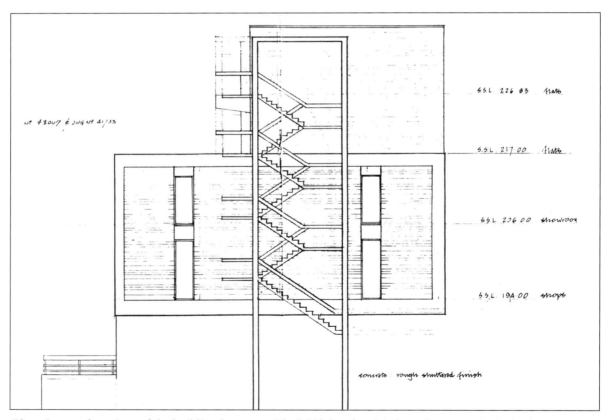

Elevations and sections of the building known as Block 'A' that faced Aylmer Square with the back towards the new Trinity Street, dated 1962.

(Mr E. Jamilly, DipArch RIBA AC Arch)

Roy Dutch's Photo Centre in West Hill in 1960 offered a wide range of cameras and photographic equipment. He later had shops at 32A Fore Street, High Cross Street and at the bottom of East Hill.

(MR R. DUTCH)

In 1894, E. Kellaway & Son were moving to a new address in Hotel Road, which was at the bottom of East Hill. (MR R. POAD)

would become the site of the telephone exchange and East Hill Garage. Lower down, Hill House Hotel, with a fountain outside, was on the junction with Eastbourne Road where the present Fountain House now stands. Further on was Penwarden's corn store, a chapel (later the British Legion), Worthington's tailors and later the Trustee Savings Bank on the corner. A brick archway at the bottom of East Hill led to Old House, in the grounds of which was a large lawn, tennis-courts and an orchard. The original ECLP offices of 1908 on High Cross Street and the company's car park later occupied part of the site. In 2005 Lidl's supermarket can be found here, and the only clue to the site's history is a large copper beech tree in the car park. Hotel Road was once the name given to the top section of road that linked East Hill with South Street.

South Street

Like East Hill, South Street has changed dramatically over time. During the early years of the twentieth-century it was the address of Moorland House School. Faraday Hall, used by the electricity company, occupied a former chapel. Kellaway's Garage was also located here, as well as Glanville's

The steam ovens inside Eustace Bakery, Eastbourne, seen in 1963. The front of the ovens rolled out on the rails to facilitate loading. These were mostly used for confectionery, while the main bread oven was more automated.

(Mr & Mrs F. Brewer)

The loading bay of Eustace Bakery, 1963.

(Mr & Mrs F. Brewer)

pasty shop which later moved to neighbouring Moorland Road. On the corner of the two roads the fine Trevail-designed terrace of houses, built in 1900, can still be seen more than 100 years later.

A significant development came about on 14 May 1974 when a Tesco superstore opened at South Street. This was to occupy a large site. They immediately provided a wide range of goods that previously would not have been available in any one shop – as well as offering double Green Shield Stamps on everything during the opening week! For example, an upright freezer could be purchased for £105, music centres were available for £99.50, while ladies' cotton or polyester dresses were only £2.25. It was not long before Tesco's faced competition from a new Asda built on the old rugby ground at Cromwell Road; there was also a weekly market at Par Moor, while shoppers at Par could visit a local branch of Gateway. All these new developments boasted large, free car parks and prices that the old shops struggled to match.

The Era of the Superstore

In 2005 all the needs of shoppers are catered for by large out-of-town shopping centres such as Tesco and Asda; the old premises in the town have given way to banks, building societies, shoe shops and charity shops. The town once boasted two bakeries: Richards & Dyer's who had a bakery in Gover Road and a shop and restaurant in Fore Street in the old Liberal Club (later Thin End), and Eustace's, with a bakery at Eastbourne and a shop on High Cross Street. These too are now consigned to history. Although there are now far fewer shoppers in the town, Fore Street is, somewhat ironically, now closed to traffic – apart from delivery vehicles and those belonging to residents with special needs.

The Decline of the Town

The decline of the town is greatly lamented by the older population in particular, who remember a thriving town centre with a wide variety of shops. Indeed, this was the situation until the end of the 1960s. Today many ask where it all went wrong. In the early 1960s when the town gained a new and modern town centre in Alymer Square, it was a vision of the future, and mirrored many such developments throughout the country. However, that vision soon turned sour; the wide open space of the square became an obstacle to shopping, while the new premises failed to hold on to established names for any length of time. An exception was Goodenough's shoe shop, who moved to Aylmer Square when their old premises were lost with the construction of Trinity Street, and remained there for many years.

However, the town's demise cannot rest solely on its 1960s' architecture; for example, a similar

This event in High Cross Street has not been recorded; it is the background that is particularly interesting, for the shops, Eustace Bakery and Rentaset TV Hire, are long gone. (MR R. DUTCH)

shopping centre at Nailsea, near Bristol, is still attractive and thriving. St Austell traders opposed large stores such as Marks & Spencer gaining a foothold in the town, short-sightedly ignoring the 'commercial magnetism' that goes hand in hand with such prestigious names. Changing needs and shopping habits, reliance on the motor car and the growth of out-of-town shopping centres have all played their part. Perhaps with the arrival of on-line shopping and grid-locked streets we are on the verge of another change.

In 2005 there is still hope for the future: St Austell looks forward to the building of a new town centre, possibly by 2007.

References

[1] *Cornish Guardian*, 29 August 1929, p.14.
[2] *Cornish Guardian*, 14 November 1927, p.9.
[3] *Cornish Guardian*, 25 April 1957, p.7.

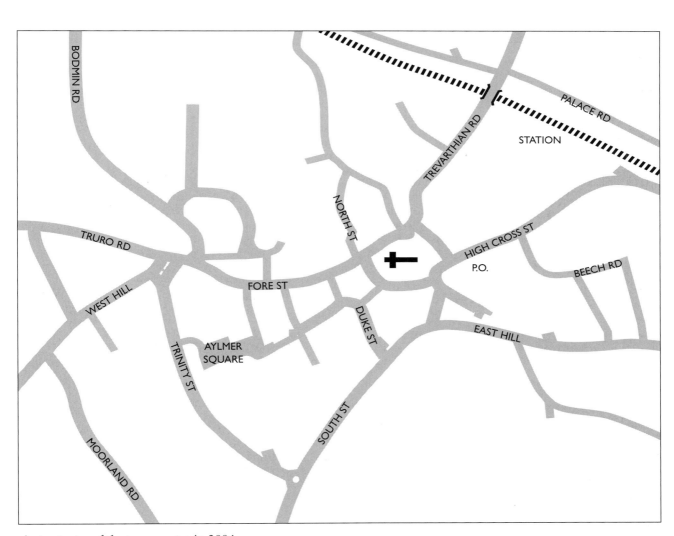

A street map of the town centre in 2004.

Chapter 3

Significant Buildings

St Austell Parish Church

St Austell boasts one of the finest churches in the South West. A church was built on the site as early as 1138. It was originally dedicated to The Holy Trinity by Bishop Bronescombe in 1259. The tower, at 96ft, is of the Somerset type and was built of Pentewan stone, as was much of the church, quarried from the cliffs at Polrudden Farm. The carvings on the western side of the tower reflect the theme of the Trinity, being in three tiers, starting with what are probably the figures of St Austell and St Mewan either side of the risen Lord. Above them, illustrating the Annunciation, are the Virgin and the angel Gabriel, separated by a vase of lilies, while at the top can be seen the Father, given greater prominence by being larger than the others, and with his hands raised to bless his Son on the cross between his cloaked legs. The other faces of the tower are decorated with carvings of the 12 apostles, while high above, beneath the battlements, grotesque animals appear to be leaping from the sides.

Parts of the older structure survive in the Chantry Chapel of St Michael off the south aisle, and are built of a different stone, taken from a quarry near Padstow. The nave and tower were constructed during the fifteenth century. The Westminster chimes were added in 1859. The tenor bell alone weighs 18½cwt.

One curious aspect of the building is the way the nave, chancel and tower are not built in a straight line; the chancel end inclines towards the north, the tower towards the south. It has been suggested that the misalignment could represent the drooping head of Christ on the cross.

Inside the church is a fine wagon roof with decorated carved-oak bosses, while the Norman font which belonged to the earlier church is decorated with carvings of the Tree of Life.

The Friends' Meeting House

This simple and inconspicuous building in High Cross Street, situated in the shadow of the retaining wall of the railway station yard, was constructed in 1834. It was paid for by the local Quaker families. Many of the gravestones beside the building were taken from the old Quaker burial-ground at Tregongeeves when the ancient site was lost to road widening in 1965. The Society of Friends had first

Holy Trinity Church, Church Street and the White Hart Hotel, viewed from the Red Bank, 1930s. The proliferation of palm trees was a feature of the churchyard as well as the railway station.

A wonderful view of Holy Trinity Church, with the Market House behind the tower, c.1935. There can be few other churchyards in the country adorned with palm trees. (Mr W. Pappin)

Holy Trinity Church, floodlit for Christmas, late 1980s. After the Second World War, St Austell was probably the first town west of Bristol to have Christmas tree lights. (Mr O. Richards)

The west front of Holy Trinity Church, c.1960.

The font.

The church doorway.

St Austell Parish Church choir outing to Bude, c.1919. Left to right, back row: *Gribble (verger), A.L. Rowse, Bob Hancock, Revd Jack Bucknall, T.W. Sandrey, Brennand Smith (organist), Harold Housman, ? Paynter, ? Truscott;* third row: *Revd Triplett, Fred ?, ? Johnson, ? Kneebone, Charles Rowe;* second row: *G. Tucker, Bertie Mably, ? Steer, Don Drake, ? Lyon, Dens Hancock, Donald Brown, Stan Tucker, ? Carne;* front row: *? Cundy, Bill Rundle, Bill Sandrey, Lionel Steer, ? Cundy, Reggie Gale, Bill Carveth, Eddy Tamblyn, Bill Hill.* (MR J. BLAKE)

Above: *The nave and south aisle of the Parish Church.*

Left: *The Chantry Chapel of St Michael, 2005.*

used the cemetery in 1664, the land being given to Thomas Lower by Richard Edgcumbe of Mount Edgcumbe Park in 1706. A slate plaque at the site states that, 'Thomas Lower became a member of the Society of Friends after visiting George Fox [the founder] when he was imprisoned in Pendennis Castle, Falmouth'. (Opposite the Friends' Meeting House is the old St Austell Cemetery, which used to be looked after by a park attendant before the graves were moved back against the wall.)

The Bible Christian Zion Church

This was partly constructed on the site of a lecture hall or Assize Hall. (Kelly's *Directory of Cornwall* for

The Bible Christian Zion Church, Trevarthian Road, a fine building but redundant in 2005.

1923 states that the County Court was held there.) The church opened in 1891 and was able to hold 600 people. However, with congregations declining it finally closed in 1994 and now this fine granite building faces an uncertain future.

St John's Wesleyan Methodist Church

This magnificent building opened in 1828 after the site in Bodmin Road was provided by the local Sawle family. In 2005, it remains an important place of worship in St Austell.

Other Places of Worship

Other places of worship within the town at the time of writing include the long-established Gospel Hall in Slades Road; St Augustine of Hippo Catholic Church in Woodland Road, the building dating from May 1990; the Church of Jesus Christ of the Latter Day Saints at Kingfisher Drive, built during the 1970s; the Seventh Day Adventists' building at Bucklers Lane; and the Church of the Holy Spirit Research and Enlightenment Centre in King's Avenue. St Austell has yet to gain a mosque.

The Workhouse

Due to the escalating cost of dealing with the poor, the Poor Law Amendment Act was passed in 1834. The Act was a means of tackling the problem by creating workhouses to feed, house and clothe

The view from the footbridge looking down Trevarthian Road, 2004. The photograph shows the Parish Church, the original brewery building with its square chimney, and the back of Zion Church.

43

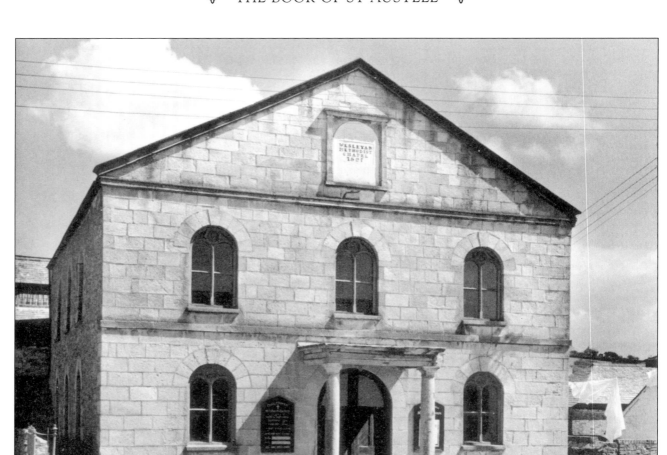

The Wesleyan Methodist chapel in Charlestown, 1960.

paupers, as well as provide them with menial work; conditions in the workhouses were to be such that all but the needy would be dissuaded from entering.

St Austell Poor Law Union was established on 2 February 1837. This catered for the town, as well as encompassing outlying parishes running from St Michael Caerhays in the south-west, in an arc through Grampound, St Stephen, St Dennis, Roche, Tywardreath and St Sampson (Golant) in the east; a total of 21 parishes with a population of over 27,000 people. The individual parishes were represented by 39 people elected to the board of guardians, who

St Blazey church, on a postcard produced by S. Dalby-Smith of St Blazey and franked January 1927.

(MRS D. BILLING)

oversaw the running of the workhouse.

The building itself was designed by the architects George Gilbert Scott and William Bonython Moffatt. It was constructed on the hill to the north of the town, on the old priory site that is the Sedgemoor Campus of St Austell College at the time of writing. The workhouse had room for 300 'inmates' and cost the Poor Law Commissioners £5,650 to build. As was the case with other workhouses, it had a symmetrical layout to ease the segregation of family members. The single-storey façade was bisected by a central archway which led to the three-storey high accommodation block. In the centre of this was the master's quarters, topped by a cupola seated between tall rectangular chimneys. A long infirmary block was located at the northern end of the site. Canon Hammond was impressed enough by the building to write; 'We have a refuge for our destitute in the shape of a really elegant Workhouse – it is of the Gothic order'.[1]

It may be interesting to look at a range of reports which throw light on a wide variety of events that occurred in the institution's long history:

The Guardians' Minute Books for 1845–8 record tenders for bread and groceries, such as 'Robert Davey's for Best Newport Coals 19s.6d. per ton', milk 'raw & scald', mutton, suet and bullocks' heads![2]

Roche church, seen in isolation, on a postcard from Argall's series, franked July 1913. Roche and St Blazey parishes came under the jurisdiction of St Austell Workhouse, along with Creed, St Dennis, St Ewe, Fowey, Gorran, Grampound, Mevagissey, St Mewan, St Michael Caerhays, St Stephen, St Sampson and Tywardreath. (Mrs D. Billing)

In February 1846 it was stated that:

The following cases were reported by the Medical Officers and relieved:

J. Polglaze	St Blazey	Ulcerated tumour
J. Williams	St Blazey	Fever
H. Phillips	Tywardreath	Inflamed liver
W. Williams	St Austell	Inflamed Kidneys
J.S. Cock	St Austell	Abscess Lungs
J. Fro ?	St Austell	Fracture of Leg[3]

Other cases that April included three more inmates suffering from fever, as well as patients with the following: an abscess, a diseased arm, a fractured leg, plus an inflamed leg and an inflamed foot.[4]

In 1860 it was reported that:

on the 1st of January – Elizabeth Rundle was... committed to prison for one calendar month, charged with absconding with cloth from St Austell Union.[5]

Not all the inmates were there because they were destitute – a number had mental health problems and would have been provided with suitable care and treatment in modern times. However, in the nineteenth century there was scant understanding of mental health. This is made clear in a report about St Austell Union in the *Royal Cornwall Gazette*, dated 1867:

Mr R.G. Lakes, as one of the visiting justices of the county asylum, called attention to the provision for persons classed under the head [sic] of imbeciles and drivelling idiots. There are about 40 in the asylum, and

it is estimated that there are altogether at least 200 in the county. In the asylum, and in most of the workhouses, this class is not kept separate from the other inmates.[6]

He went on to highlight the problems faced by other inmates, when housed with those suffering from mental illnesses. As a result a separate ward was contemplated.

At a dinner at the White Hart Hotel in March 1901 the chairman of the St Austell board of guardians said that the guardians had paid £5,300 in 'out-relief' (i.e. poor law relief outside the workhouse), £2,578 for lunatics, which together with the cost of 'in-maintenance' (within the workhouse) meant that the expenditure for the previous year amounted to £11,343. He also mentioned that a new infirmary was to be built, and as the result of the good work that the board had done 'was delighted to find that the number of able-bodied paupers in the House was growing less and less'.[7]

In 1918 it was reported that 'St Austell Board of Guardians has appointed Mr and Mrs J. Partridge, of Southampton, as master and matron of the work-house, and Miss Kent, Nanpean, as foster-mother'.[8]

By 1929 a total of 130 people were housed in the workhouse. During that year the staff also had to contend with an outbreak of influenza:

Dr Marshall, chairman of the House Committee, reported an outbreak of influenza in the Institution. About 50 inmates were ill and several members of the staff were affected. He drew the attention of the Board to the fact that in consequence the work in the House was getting extremely difficult. To take the temperature of all those inmates took a nurse between two and three hours. The work of the staff had been very much increased through the outbreak.[9]

The article in the local paper went on to say: 'The Master (Mr F. Cooper) reported that 33 vagrants were relieved for the fortnight against 21 for the corresponding fortnight last year'.[10]

Dr Marshall also raised concerns expressed by the board that the heating system had become obsolete and recommended that a new system should be installed.

Housing Issues

Even if people managed to escape the tyranny of the workhouse, their domestic situation was often little better. In 1904 there were reports of overcrowding in a house near the Council School, Mount Charles:

There were three adults and seven children all of whom had recently left the Union. The House was clean, but contained scarcely any furniture. The house contained two small bedrooms, 14ft by 10ft by 8ft, and 9ft by 8ft by 8ft.[11]

The following report cited a similar case:

At Porthpean-road [sic], in another cottage, were Louisa Richards and her two children. She also had recently left the Workhouse. The house was devoid of furniture, and a bundle of straw in the upstair [sic] room served the purpose of a bed.[12]

The Market House

The original Market House opposite the church was built during the seventeenth century, and dealt in farm produce, while fish and meat were sold outside. It was replaced in 1791, and the present building, intended to double as a market hall and the Town Hall, was constructed of local granite by Messrs Olvers of Falmouth from the designs of Cope and Eales of London. It was completed in 1844 at a cost of £7,000.

The Market House during the 1850s.

Inside the entrance, under a substantial vaulted ceiling, was an area set aside for the sale of farm produce. Then there was a meat market in the centre of the ground floor.

Stone stairways on either side lead up to the first floor. It is worth looking at the old display board of fees above the left stairwell, as well as the amazing timbered roof, fashioned from yellow pine, the main beams of which are over 50ft long. It is claimed to be the largest unsupported single-span wooden roof in Europe. The interior of the Market House has been adapted and changed for various functions over the years. Upstairs was originally the Town Hall, until it was converted into a cinema in about 1914. This had a hand-operated projector for showing silent films, with musical accompaniment provided by somebody playing a piano. The front portion of the first floor later became a dance hall, colloquially dubbed 'Hell's Kitchen'. Locals recall that there were occasionally fights outside it on Saturday nights. This part of the first floor also served as the regional branch of the Amalgamated Engineering Union; it is the site of Evans's hardware store in 2005.

There was also a fire station on the first floor, which was level with the road on the north side of the building. This housed a horse-drawn fire-engine which was operated by a hand pump. A fire bell once hung inside a wooden tower above the entrance.

In addition to its function as a market hall, the building was also a meeting place. Both William Ewart Gladstone and Winston Churchill spoke to large crowds from its gallery.

In 1894 the Market House was the venue for the Grand Indian Palace Bazaar, an extravaganza organised to raise money for the construction of the new Young Men's Christian Association (YMCA) building then being constructed on the site of the Ring o' Bells

The Market House, c.1960.

Details of the opening ceremony of the Grand Indian Palace Bazaar in 1894.

(MR R. POAD)

Inn at Vicarage Place. The new building was to include reading-rooms, secretaries' offices, a gymnasium, library and correspondence rooms, classrooms and lecture hall; the estimated cost of completing the work was £2,895. It was hoped that the building would meet the aims of the association which were stated in the souvenir handbook as the promotion of the spiritual, intellectual, social and physical welfare of all young men, by means of Bible classes, lectures, debates, educational classes and physical exercise.

The bazaar was opened by Francis Barrett JP CC. An illusion of a magnificent palace had been created, with terraced gardens overlooking the sacred Ganges; it was described by the enthusiastic author of the handbook as follows:

The whole, flooded with glorious light of an Eastern sun, conveys at a glance an impression that is calculated to outlive whole volumes of descriptive literature.

An additional tableau, 'The Palace and Garden of Electra', opened by Mrs Tremayne of Heligan, was used to demonstrate various forms of electric lighting, cooking and heating, provided by Messrs Veale & Co. Ltd of St Austell. There were also stalls selling flowers, plants and pottery, as well as a programme of music and an Italian puppet show for children to enjoy.

Looking down Market Square, past the Market House and the Queen's Head Hotel on the right, with the church railings behind the wonderful old gas lamp, 1920s.

(MR W. PAPPIN)

Dr A.L. Rowse described a visit to the Market House during the period between the two world wars when he was a boy:

Avoiding the butchers' standings below, with the fearsome carcasses hanging in subterranean gloom, I went up the steps to the dazzling brilliance, the hissing gas-lamps, the flaring jets of upstairs... I remember the sensation to the eyes of so much dazzle after the semi-darkness of the vaulted crypt below... 'Market' was for me almost entirely a feast of the eyes and ears, for the whole of the vast space (there was no vaster known to my experience) buzzed with the excitement of a high-spirited Cornish crowd out to enjoy itself after the week's work, the sibilant murmur of a hundred conversations, the shrill cries of the stall-holders, the higgling and haggling of customers.[13]

The Odeon Cinema

The building of a new 1,200-seat cinema in St Austell was first announced in the *Cornish Guardian* on 11 April 1935. It was designed by the Odeon chain's specialist architect, Harry Weedon, in the then popular art deco style, like its contemporary, the liner *Queen Mary*. Constructed by a local firm belonging to John Williams, it was completed in 1936. At the time it provided the town with a state-of-the-art facility, with a contemporary design and using the latest technology. Marking its opening the *Cornish Guardian* was full of praise: 'The Odeon is an imposing building. A prominent feature is the slab tower with projecting faience fin, the whole lighted with Neon tubes'.[14]

The neon signs – twin tubes of green – and lighting had been installed by Bassett's of Bodmin, who also maintained them. The Odeon signs were painted red with gold leaf on the edges.

The inside of the building was described thus: 'It is laid out and equipped on the most modern lines, and there have been introduced the latest devices and amenities known to the cinema world'.[15]

Oscar Deutsch, the governing director of Odeon Theatres Ltd, attended the grand opening on 11 July 1936. The inaugural event was described as follows:

The opening of the Odeon cinema theatre on Saturday night was characterised by a brilliant scene when the huge building, with its seating capacity of 1,258, was filled with an admiring audience.[16]
Mr Oscar Deutsch, after thanking Mr Bragg [Chairman of St Austell Urban District Council], paid a tribute to the builders and architect, who had given them 'this beautiful building'.[17]

Mr Bragg also praised the work of the builders and said it was a matter of regret that:

... the work was completed because it involved the

unemployment of the men who worked there, but they might be consoled by the fact that Messrs Williams had recently received the contract for the erection of over a hundred houses at St Blazey...[18]

It was not long before the outbreak of the Second World War. During this period the cinema was painted in camouflage colours and fire watchers were stationed on the roof. Outside, posters were displayed encouraging people to contribute towards the £5,000 needed for a Spitfire, to be named in the town's honour. Films were shown to boost the flagging wartime morale, while newsreels provided vital news and information.[19]

After the war 'the Odeon Circle' provided Saturday entertainment for children, who were encouraged to sing 'We are members of the Odeon Circle, happy boys and girls are we...' Before the film began, the cinema manager, dressed in a suit and bow tie, would address his young audience from the stage.

Children were often allowed in to see A-certificate (adults only) films if accompanied by an adult, and could often stay for several hours as the programme of films was repeated.

In 1967 the name of the cinema was changed to The Classic. Then in 1978 it became known as St Austell Film Centre. In 2005 it is known as The Filmcentre, but is likely to be demolished in the near future as part of the new town centre development.

St Austell Brewery Company

Anyone who visits St Austell will be struck by the large number of public houses in and around the town. This is due to the presence of the St Austell Brewery Company. The smells that emanate from its premises on Trevarthian Road on days when brewing is done are familiar to local residents, as was the hooter that marked significant times such as the start of the working day, 'crib' (break), lunch and the end of the working day, until its strident sound ceased in the year 2000.

It is difficult to determine how many alehouses existed in St Austell up until the nineteenth century, as brewing would often take place in the back rooms of cottages, and the drink prepared for favoured visitors. Such was the case with the premises known as the Seven Stars at the bottom of East Hill, acquired by one Walter Hicks in 1863. This business was unable to satisfy his ambitions, so he bought the London Inn on Market Street and in 1869 developed the site to create a new 'steam' brewery in what is known as Tregonissey House in 2005. The stout granite chimney still hints at its past, while it is said that at night the upper storeys have an eerie presence and the scent of hops can still be detected. Steam was used to heat the mash, as well as providing the power for pumping spring water to

the building from a well.

The business was a success. By 1893 Hicks had leased the site further to the north of the town towards the hamlet of Tregonissey, which remains the location of the business in 2005. He employed the London architects Inskipp and Mackenzie to design the new building. By then he had acquired 20 pubs throughout the county (as well as in Tavistock) as outlets for his products. Later the dominant brick tower was added, along with further additions in 1914. The eponymous name of the business was changed to the St Austell Brewery Company in 1934. It remains an independent family firm in 2005, with many of Walter Hick's descendants being involved in the business.

St Austell's Public Houses

Carlyon Arms, Sandy Bottom. Nicholas Pascoe was the landlord in 1881. By 1923 the landlord was Tom Stone. The pub was purchased by St Austell Brewery in 1929 for £850.

Charlestown Hotel was built in 1793. As early as 1800 it had its own malting house on the other side of the harbour, but this facility was demolished in 1895 following the undermining of its foundations during a storm which damaged part of the outer harbour wall. The landlord in 1830 was Richard Collihole. However, once the Rashleigh Arms had been built, the hotel stopped trading and became a farm. It was also a boarding-house before reopening under a new name: **Pier House Hotel.**

Cottage Inn, Holmbush. The landlord in 1858 was George Inch, but by 1873 it was being run by John White.

Duke of Cornwall Hotel, Mount Charles, was run by John Rowse in 1873. It was bought by Walter Hicks in 1889 for £2,800. Freddie Titmuss, the Plymouth Argyle full-back from the 1920s, ran it after he retired.

Fountain Inn, Truro Road. This hostelry was established in 1822. Rebecca Nott ran it in 1830. It was demolished in about 1847.

Golden Lion, 10 Church Street. This establishment was run by John Bawden in 1830, John Ball in 1852/53 and James Truscott in 1873. In 1900 it was leased by Walter Hicks. Daniel Beadle was the landlord in 1923. In 1928 St Austell Brewery purchased the freehold; in 1933 they demolished the premises and rebuilt the pub on the same site.

Graham's Arms, Hotel Road.

Harbourside Inn, Charlestown. This establishment opened in 2004 utilising the old garage of the Pier House Hotel and replacing the previous inn that had been made from the converted lounge/café.

Holmbush Inn. In 1873 it was run by Mrs Mary Jane Thomas. The business was purchased by St Austell Brewery in 1929 for £900. A programme of refurbishment during the 1980s transformed it from a quiet traditional pub into one that is popular with a younger clientele.

King's Arms. This was run by Hannah Gilbert in 1830, but was demolished to make way for the Market House, c.1844.

King's Head. The proprietor was Walter Giles in 1830. By 1852/53 William Tredinnick was landlord.

London Inn, Market Street, was run by Jeremiah Lark in 1830. It was sold at auction by Hancock & Sons on 21 May 1867. The advertisement read as follows:

The said Inn and Premises stand on a large area of ground, and contain Sixteen Rooms, besides a large cellar, a commodious and convenient Brew House, large Stable and Loft over the same, a Yard with convenient Out Offices.[20]

The pub was bought by Walter Hicks who developed it into his brewery at Tregonissey House.

Mennear's Temperance Hotel, Market Hill. This was a popular retreat for farmers seeking a meal on market-day, or for commercial travellers needing somewhere to stay while on business in the town. The hotel was destroyed by fire in 1925.

Mount Charles Inn. For many years this establishment was run by the Inch family. In 1871 it was let, along with an adjoining cooperage. According to Kelly's *Directory of Cornwall* for 1893, the landlord was Daniel Sampson, who was also a cooper.

Ring o' Bells (Ringing Bells), Victoria Square, was run by William Minear in 1830 and William Boase in 1852/53. Joseph Warne was there in 1873, when it was acquired by Walter Hicks. In 1892 it was sold and subsequently demolished to be replaced by the YMCA building in 1893 (as described in the section on the Market House earlier in this chapter). Prior to this the landlord had been R. Huddy who was also operating as a hairdresser; a butcher's shop also occupied part of the premises.

Sun Inn, Market Street. In 1830 it was run by John Julyan, and then John Hodge for over 20 years, whose entry in Kelly's *Directory of Cornwall* for 1873 also listed him as a nursery and seedsman, for which he also had premises in Fore Street. The inn was sold in 1909 to Walter Hicks for £1,150 when it was auctioned by Messrs Hancock & Sons. In 1923 William Thomas was the landlord. In 2005, it is the site of an Irish bar called O'Callaghan's.

The Dolphin Inn, overlooking the beach at Porthpean. This was bought and extended by the Petherick family and later became the private residence known as Porthpean House.

The General Wolfe. This inn was constructed c.1785 on what was then known as Wainhouse Corner on Fore Street. It was run by the Penticosts during the eighteenth century, then Joseph Gawler and, following his death, his wife. Thomas May ran it in 1830. In 1852/53 John Skewes was landlord, in 1873 John Job, and in 1923, Bramble George Olver. It closed in 2002 and the site is part of Adeba Toys in 2005.

The Globe Hotel was situated on what is now Truro Road; it was built on the site of the Fountain Inn c.1847, before Truro Road existed. The hotel was a convenient stopping place for coaches on their way from Launceston or Bodmin to Truro using the North Street and West Hill route. Recorded as being run by Ann Gillies in 1852 and a Miss Carhart in 1873, it was part of the Penrice estate until acquired by Walter Hicks in 1892. However, in 1904 the licence was refused so it became redundant. It was then taken over by John Warne and his son Frederick, the founders of the printing works and stationery business which flourished there for over 50 years. Four generations of the Warne family would trade

The bottom of East Hill, showing the Seven Stars and the White Hart Hotel in the 1950s. The white building on the corner was once the Trustee Savings Bank before becoming the premises of Roy Dutch Photo Centre. This notorious corner, responsible for catching out many unwary lorry drivers, was bypassed by a new stretch of road during the 1980s. (MR R. DUTCH)

The Duke of Cornwall Hotel, Mount Charles, 1920s. The shop on the left has disappeared, to make way for road widening. (Mr W. Pappin)

there before transferring to new premises at East Hill/Albert Road

The Golden Fleece. This was run by Peter Crapp in 1764, who was recorded as being a tin merchant as well as a 'maltster'.

The Hideaway, Porthpean. This small pub on the cliffs above the beach was only turned into a private residence in the 1980s.

The New Inn, Fore Street and Chandos Place. This establishment was run by John Bray in 1830 and Henry Stephens in 1852/53. It was demolished during the 1960s as part of the town's redevelopment. It was situated behind present-day Woolworth's.

The Queen's Head Hotel, Fore Street. This hotel dates from 1740 and is one of the oldest buildings in St Austell. It was originally an alehouse. A tunnel is said to run from the cellar to the old

brewery, or even Porthpean, while the ghost of a chambermaid called Bessie haunts the building. Landlords from 1830 to 1903 included Jane Tallack, Richard Trounce, Joseph Toms and William Philp.

The Rashleigh Arms, Charlestown. James Truscott was landlord in 1830. By 1851 Thomas Stephens was the proprietor. It was a free-house until St Austell Brewery purchased it.

The Seven Stars, Hotel Road/East Hill. Elizabeth Phillips ran the establishment in 1830, but by 1852/53 Ann Annear was landlady. Walter Hicks bought the lease in 1863 for £550, but in 1925 St Austell Brewery purchased the freehold for £1,000. It was run by William Tyzzer in 1923.

The Stag Inn, Victoria Place. In 1830 Nicholas May was landlord, William Ham in 1852/53, and by 1873 the landlord was James Hooper.

The Western Inn, Western Road. In 1830 the landlord was Robert May. By 1852/53 John Penna had taken over. It was run by the Treluswell Brewery Company until the leasehold was purchased by St Austell Brewery in 1943 for £2,500. They purchased the freehold in 1962 for £1,250.

The White Hart Hotel was once situated in Fore Street. The site of the present hotel was once the town house of Charles Rashleigh. Elizabeth Price was the proprietor in 1830 and Robert Dunn in 1852/53. It was bought by Walter Hicks in 1911 for £5,000. In 1925/26 the building was raised from two to three storeys. It underwent a major refurbishment in 2003.

White Lion, in the Bull Ring. It was demolished to make way for The Red Bank.

William Cookworthy, at Tregonissey, was built by St Austell Brewery in 1969 for £36,343 and is the only modern purpose-built pub in the town. Extremely popular with young people during the 1980s, it was later refurbished as a family bar and restaurant. In 2005 it is a training centre for St Austell Brewery.

This block of houses once included the White Lion Inn on the right-hand side, before it was demolished to make way for The Red Bank commissioned by Coode & Shilson in 1897. The old Corn Exchange is on the corner next to the White Hart Hotel, and is seen from the churchyard. Three small shops once stood beneath the fence in what was known as the Bull Ring, probably because cattle were once gathered there for market. (Mr R. Dutch)

? Inn. No.21, Charlestown Road, Charlestown. A private residence at the time of writing, this small cottage next to the dock was once an inn and no doubt frequented by sailors and dock workers.

Silvanus Trevail

Silvanus Trevail was probably the town's greatest architect. He was born at Luxulyan in October 1851. His education began at Luxulyan village school, before he attended Ledrah House School in St Austell. He trained as an architect in London, completing his studies under the tutelage of the prominent London architect, Henry Garling, before returning to Cornwall in 1872.

His first commission in that year was the Elementary Board School at Mount Charles. It was designed to accommodate 375 pupils and was completed at a cost of £945. He was also responsible for the design of a number of other schools in the area, including the Central School on West Hill in 1873 which, following the 1870 Education Act, replaced an earlier one that had been established in 1832 as a National School. The buildings were demolished in 1999 to be replaced by the College Green/Trinity Street housing scheme, following the construction of a new tax office on the old football pitch. Other schools in Trevail's portfolio include St Mewan, Fowey Board School in 1876, and Carclaze

Mount Charles Wesleyan Methodist chapel, designed by Silvanus Trevail and constructed in 1873. No longer serving modern requirements, it was demolished in 1995 to make way for a new version. (MRS H. HARRADENCE)

School in 1878. Treverbyn School, which he designed in 1876, was sold for redevelopment in December 2003, although many campaigned to have the building demolished so that the site could provide a larger car park for the new junior school.

In 1879 Trevail branched out into designing hotels. Of the 12 that he worked on probably the most noteworthy are the Great Western in Newquay, the Star and Castle at St Mawes and King Arthur's Castle at Tintagel.

An example of Trevail's attention to detail can be seen in his designs for St Austell Liberal Club, opened in 1890, which included interior friezes as well as alternative balustrades for the staircase, on top of the riot of design on the exterior façades.[21] Above the shops on the ground floor were reading- and smoking-rooms (which form the Thin End Restaurant in 2005), while a billiard room was located on the second floor which was the venue for dances during the Second World War.

Similar attention to detail was given to The Red Bank. Gable façades were created to face each of the three approaches, while the terracotta stone that gave the building its name came from Ruabon in North Wales. It was commissioned by Messrs Coode and Shilson in 1897.

Another Silvanus Trevail building of great significance for the town, but with a completely different character, was the St Austell Public Rooms, of 1894 (described in more detail below).[22] In sharp contrast to the bank, this solid looking building, Courts furniture store until 2004, was constructed of sombre granite.

Ecclesiastical work included the Wesleyan chapel, Mount Charles, in 1872; the renovation of the interiors of the Congregational Church and St John's Wesleyan Church; and designs for proposed cemetery chapels for Mevagissey and St Austell Burial Boards.

Other Trevail designs around the town are a terrace of houses on the corner of South Street and Moorland Road commissioned by Francis Leyland Barratt JP – a plaque on the wall of the lower gable reads 'F L B 1900' – and so-called 'workmen's dwellings' further along Moorland Road, also for Barratt. The two men had previously collaborated on Tregarne Terrace in 1894.

At Trenython, near Tywardreath, Trevail designed an entrance lodge and a private chapel for the bishop of Truro. The unassuming terrace of houses next to the old cemetery on High Cross Street was created for J.E. Veale JP in 1901 and served as police houses for the neighbouring Police Station.

Silvanus Trevail's work was not just confined to St Austell. He had a close association with the philanthropist, Passmore Edwards, and designed many buildings for him throughout Devon and Cornwall, as well as the Passmore Edwards Library and Hospital at East Ham, London. Other work outside

the county ranged from Woodside Mansion in Dublin and The Grand Hotel, Guernsey.

Trevail had offices at 66–68 Lemon Street, Truro, where he was assisted by the architect Alfred Cornelius. He in turn was responsible for the design of Pon-Dhu Cottages in 1892. Mr A. Wells took over Cornelius's practice in December 1964.

Besides running his architect's practice, Trevail was also involved in local affairs. He was made borough councillor for Truro in November 1886 and Mayor in 1894–95. He was also a magistrate.

Perhaps he took on too much. Tragically, in 1903, while travelling in a train from Truro, he shot himself in the head with a revolver at the point where the track passed through Brown Queen tunnel near Bodmin Road station. At his inquest the coroner's verdict was that 'business worries' had led to his suicide.

He was buried with his parents in Luxulyan churchyard, his grave marked by a granite cross that he had designed the previous year. In 1906 his only sister, Laura, commissioned a stained-glass window for the church in his honour.

St Austell Public Rooms

Designed by Silvanus Trevail, and constructed in 1894, this fine building was used for a wide variety of purposes, including meetings, dances, functions, music festivals, etc. On 10 August 1904, General

The splendid Masonic Hall, facing Duke Street, creates a dramatic backdrop to a parade. The old church hall and Sunday school is on the right. Frank Law's tobacconist advertises Player's cigarettes. (Mr R. Dutch)

Booth, founder of the Salvation Army, gave a lecture there, the title of which was 'Lessons of Life, as Illustrated by the Spiritual and Social Work of the Army'.[23] During the 1930s a Dennis fire-engine was housed on the ground floor, and alerted by the tenor bell in the church tower. Various businessmen in the town – such as Mr Nicholls from the jeweller's, Mc Turk's the baker opposite Woolworth's, Mr Stephens from Smith's Corner, Herbert Rowse the auctioneer, and Mr Sanders the builder – were collected from their premises on the way. It was later converted into Courts furniture store, as it remained until 2004.

The Masonic Hall, South Street

The hall was designed by the architect F.C. Jury and was completed in 1900 at a cost of £998. The grand late-Victorian façade facing the entrance to Duke Street is full of symbolism that is lost on many. On the top of the gable is a pentagonal star, and beneath it the Masonic square and compass. This surmounts an arch which encircles the arms of the United Grand Lodge of England, supported by two doves bearing olive branches. On either side of the door, elegant pillars support a sturdy lintel decorated with more Masonic symbols. The windows are of stained glass, while inside the temple is magnificently decorated in bright colours.

References
[1] Canon Joseph Hammond, *A Cornish Parish: Being an Account of St Austell, Town, Church, District and People*, p.3.
[2] The Guardians' Minute Book of St Austell Workhouse, 1845–8, p.332, (held at Cornwall Record Office, Truro – PU St Austell 3).
[3] *Ibid.*, p.97.
[4] *Ibid.*, p.128.
[5] *Royal Cornwall Gazette*, 13 January 1860, p.5.
[6] *Royal Cornwall Gazette*, 9 May 1867, p.8.
[7] *Cornish Guardian*, 29 March 1901, p.2.
[8] *Royal Cornwall Gazette*, 4 September 1918, p.6.
[9] *Cornish Guardian*, 21 February 1929, p.14.
[10] *Ibid.*
[11] *Cornish Guardian*, 29 July 1904, p.2.
[12] *Ibid.*
[13] A.L. Rowse, *A Cornish Childhood*, p.12–13.
[14] *Cornish Guardian*, 16 July 1936, p.7.
[15] *Ibid.*
[16] *Ibid.*
[17] *Ibid.*
[18] *Ibid.*
[19] Peter Hancock, *Cornwall at War*.
[20] *Royal Cornwall Gazette*, 16 May 1867, p.5.
[21] Extant plans held at Cornwall Record Office, Truro (A.D.396/161).
[22] *Ibid.* (A.D.396/162 & 182).
[23] *Cornish Guardian*, 22 July 1904, p.5.

Chapter 4

A Clay Town

A Brief History of the China Clay Industry

The quest for 'white gold' in the district began in 1748 when William Cookworthy, a Plymouth chemist, discovered deposits of china clay in the area. Two years earlier he had found the kaolin (also known as china clay) he sought to make fine porcelain close to Tregonning Hill, near Helston.

It was not long before the main pottery families had acquired their own clay works to supply their raw materials. Treviscoe Pit, the first one to be operational, was established by Wedgewood, and by 1814 there were six others, run by Spode, Minton and others. However, over the years Cornish families took over the operations – the Martyn family buying Treviscoe – so that by the 1870s there were around 120 independent companies. Gradually some of the pits were worked out, or companies merged. The most significant of these liaisons occurred in 1919 when the West of England China Clay Company, Martyn Brothers, and North Cornwall China Clays joined to form English China Clays Co. in an operation that then accounted for 50 per cent of the output of china clay.

In 1932 English Clay Lovering Pochin (ECLP & Co. Ltd) was created when English China Clays Ltd acquired John Lovering and H.D. Pochin. Despite gaining international interests they remained a local company, with their head offices at John Keay House, until their merger with the French mineral company IMETAL (later Imerys) in 1999.

In 2005 only one independent producer remains in Cornwall, Goonvean Ltd, which operates four pits.

Wheal Par mine, c.1890.

Other companies came under the ECLP umbrella, including joiners John Williams Ltd; The Wheal Remfry China Clay, Brick & Tile Co. Ltd; Heavy Transport Ltd; Western Express Haulage Ltd; Western Excavating Ltd; and Charlestown Engineering Ltd. (The latter finally closed at the end of September 2004 after 181 years of trading.)

After leasing Par Harbour for 18 years, ECLP bought this important facility in 1964. Fowey's port was taken over in 1968 and the railway line that had served it since the 1920s was converted to a road linking the two harbours. Clay shipments from Charlestown continued, but the small tidal harbour was growing increasingly inconvenient and shipments finally came to a close during the 1990s.

The Clay Industry and Employment

The china clay industry has always been a major employer in the area. A total of 3,746 people were working in the industry in 1937.[1] In 1947 just over 4,000 people were employed.[2] This rose to a peak during the 1960s, with approximately 8,000 employed in 1965.[3] However, over the years the industry has become more mechanised, and new methods of refining have been introduced so that the local industry has been able to remain competitive in a global market. In 2003 a total of 2,133 people in Cornwall were employed by Imerys,[4] in a diverse range of positions including production operatives, laboratory technicians, scientists – there was even a shepherd!

Nor should the many ancillary industries that provide employment be forgotten; it is estimated that over 20 per cent of the population of Restormel is supported by incomes from the china clay industry.[5]

Clearly the industry has been a huge boost to the local economy which would otherwise have had to rely on tourism, agriculture and small businesses. In fact, when taking the procurement of goods and services, wages and local taxes into account, over £80 million was injected into the local economy during 2002.[6]

The Clay Workers' Strike of 1913

In 1911 a full-time trade union organiser, Mr C.A. Vincent, was appointed in the St Austell area; he acquired an office in South Street. In June 1912, against a background of national strikes on the railways and in the coal mines, the Workers' Union supported the clay workers when they made four demands: a standard eight-hour day with an hour's

53

The staff of John Williams, 1974.   (Mr R. Bassett)

Wheal Remfry brickworks.   (Imerys)

The John Williams building before its demise, and Pentewan Roundabout, c.1982.   (Mr R. Sandercock)

The Heavy Transport fleet of lorries photographed in front of the Pier House Hotel, Charlestown, 1934/5. Their depot was behind the hotel.   (Mr A. Deller)

The clay ship Lantic Bay *entering the inner harbour at Charlestown, late-twentieth century.* (Mr M. Stone)

A gathering to mark the closing of Greensplatt clay works in 1959, where the last beam engine in the county to work commercially was finally shut down. (Sometimes the village name is spelt Greensplatt.)

(Mr R. Dutch)

lunch break; fortnightly payments instead of monthly; a minimum basic wage of 25s. a week; and for the clay companies to recognise the union.

There was growing unrest in the china clay industry during the early months of 1913. At the time the average wage of a china clay worker was less than £1 (or 20s.) a week. The china clay companies were reluctant to increase wages and were averse to recognising the increasing militancy amongst the workers, coupled with a growing allegiance to the trade unions.

Most of the clay companies were slow to respond, and it was not long before the situation reached crisis point. The *Cornish Guardian* noted on 21 February 1913 that:

No one who has any knowledge from the inside of what is now happening in the clay industry so far as the wages question is concerned can longer doubt the gravity which is taking hold of the situation. On the one hand the companies, I am afraid, have not quite grasped the realities of the position.

With the workers finding it increasingly hard to make ends meet, and the clay companies unwilling to conciliate, the reporter went on to add: 'One thing is quite certain now – that the men are beginning to assert themselves'.[7]

The situation cannot have been helped by the buoyant economy in the clay industry at the time, and it was clear that the clay companies could have conceded to the men's demands. This would have been apparent to anyone who read the local *Cornish Guardian* on 9 May 1913 (p.6) when it commented on a report in the *Cornish Mining Notes and News* that mentioned a china clay boom:

To meet the phenomenal demand which now exists for this much used commodity old works are undertaking great extensions and developments, while new works are bringing fresh clay lands into service.[8]

Things came to a head in July. The *Cornish Guardian* reported on the latest developments under the headline 'Companies' Rises Delay Strike':

Under the auspices of the Workers' Union another enthusiastic meeting was held in the open air at St Austell on Saturday evening, when the principal subjects dealt with were the ultimatum presented to the clay merchants demanding a minimum wage of 25s. per week, and the rise of 1s.6d. per week by the West of England Co., which was claimed by the speakers to be the result of the agitation.

Mr C.R. Vincent, local organiser, in a speech frequently punctuated with applause, reviewed the circumstances which led up to the Union's present action. Prior to the advent of the Union eighteen months before the wages of 2,000 of the 4,000 clay workers in Mid-Cornwall were 18s. per week. He recalled the fact that soon after the agitation for an advance began, a bonus of 2d. or 3d. per day was

Dorothy clay works, at Whitemoor during the 1920s. The picture shows the double incline to the top of the sky tip, the sand drags below, and the engine house on the right. Mrs Dulcie Billing, who kindly supplied the picture, recalls climbing the incline with her friends during the Second World War when the works were closed.

(Mrs D. Billing)

Kernick clay works, St Stephen, showing the mica drags and settling tanks, 1920s.

(Mrs D. Billing)

Left: *A view of Burngullow showing the settling pits and mica drags, 1920s. In 2005 the area is dominated by Blackpool china-clay works to the north.*

(Mrs D. Billing)

Trenance Siding, St Austell, 1920s. The location of the siding, next to the main line, meant it was convenient for dispatching the processed china clay.

(Mrs D. Billing)

Left: *English China Clays Ltd, St Austell, is clearly displayed on the sides of the railway wagons standing before the china clay kilns (or dries) at Kernick, St Stephen, 1920s. These were divided into two parts, the 'pan' or drying kiln, and at a lower level the 'linhay' or storage area.*

(Mrs D. Billing)

An evocative picture showing the loading of china stone at the wharves of Quarry Close, St Stephen, during the period between the two world wars. There were four classes of china stone produced by ECC Ltd: hard purple, mild purple, white and buff. The first was highly esteemed by the potter, as it was almost an essential constituent of glaze or enamel mixtures. The mild purple and white were next in favour, while the buff was used primarily as a binder in body work.

(Mrs D. Billing)

This house at Trenance, St Austell was once occupied by the 'Captain' of Carrancarrow clay works. At one time English China Clays Ltd also had about 400 cottages in the St Austell district. (MRS D. BILLING)

conceded by all the companies. They claimed that the bonus was given because of the introduction of Trade Unionism in the area...[9]

The union then announced that they thought it was time for more drastic action to be taken. As a result:

In accordance with Rule 11 of the Workers' Union they approached the Executive for permission to lay 'down tools' in order to enforce the demands of the petition.[10]

The following week a meeting was called at the Public Rooms in St Austell. A resolution was passed that 'all men not having received an increase [were] at once to tender their notices, through the Workers' Union, to withdraw their labour'. And if their terms were not met, they were 'at a later date to 'down tools' all hands'.[11]

The resolve of the clay workers must have been

hardened by another inflammatory article in the *Cornish Guardian*, this time commenting on a report that had recently been published in the *Financial News*, stating:

The unprecedented demand for china clay continues unabated... [any prospector can] command a cash price that will reward him well as seller, and ensure for the capitalist a splendid return on his outlay.[12]

Soon the strike was becoming a reality. By 24 July the *Royal Cornwall Gazette* reported:

On Tuesday there were 25 men out... and on Thursday there would be 150, and it was only necessary to give the word and many hundreds would go on strike.[13]

The next day in the *Cornish Guardian* the following was reported:

Matters came to a head so far as one section of the clay workers are concerned on Monday when some of the employes [sic] of the Carne Stents clay works came out on strike.

Rescrowsa Farm, Nanpean, showing one of the horses and carts, 1920s. Quite a number of horses were employed in farm work as well as for haulage. (MRS D. BILLING)

English China Clays Ltd also had its own farm, at Rescrowsa, Nanpean, where many horses were kept for hauling loads of china clay. Some of the horses were brought over from Canada during the First World War.

(MRS D. BILLING)

Gradually horses gave way to motorised transport. Seen here is a 5-ton Halford tipping lorry with solid tyres and chain drive, used for carrying coal etc., to various works from Drinnick Mill Station some time after the First World War. (MRS D. BILLING)

Carclaze Clay Pit, showing the incline to the top of the pit, early-twentieth century.

Carclaze Clay Pit (pictured here in the early-twentieth century) was for many years something of a tourist attraction for early travellers. To those unfamiliar with the Clay Country, apart from its spectacular size, it certainly had an extra-terrestrial appearance.

This, one of the smaller clay companies, had 'declined to accede to the request' for an increase in wages, causing most of their employees to lose patience and initiate the strike.[14] There followed an incident when the men who had downed tools threw stones at those who had rejected Mr Vincent's request and carried on working. If this continued, the captain prophetically said, he would have to 'seek police protection'.[15] They were followed by 50 clay workers at Penhale, while at Gunheath, 'the men decided to go on strike, but afterwards gave the company until Saturday to consider a rise in wages'.[16]

By the beginning of August the strike had not spread beyond the smaller works, and some strikers had actually returned to work or were contemplating a return. However, following a Workers' Union meeting at the Public Rooms, when they re-affirmed their demands, on the following Monday morning the Workers' Union officials, Messrs Matt Giles and C.R. Vincent, accompanied by police to keep the peace, walked from pit to pit with a group of strikers drumming up support. Undaunted by the hot summer weather, they visited other pits over the following days, with the result that within a short time some 95 per cent of all the pits were closed. By 7 August production was only continuing at Carclaze, Garker, Wheal Hope and Hallew. However, following some persuasion, as well as a

certain amount of threats and intimidation, Carclaze and Garker fell into line. At Wheal Hope some of the mens' clothes and tools were burnt, while more drastic action was taken at the house of one of the shift bosses at Hallew: 'A charge of dynamite in a tin can was exploded, breaking a number of windows, and frightening the women and children'.[17]

There were other minor incidents elsewhere as people took sides and animosity developed. The *Royal Cornwall Gazette* noted:

The clay district of Cornwall is in a state of chaos... The state of affairs is appalling and the position of the men and their families is becoming daily more acute from the fact that little or no money is coming in to furnish the larder with the necessities of life.[18]

It was not long before police reinforcements were called for. Up until this point relationships between the strikers and the police had been good. After all, the police were local men and often sympathised with the plight of the clay workers. At the end of August 190 reinforcements were brought in, including 100 specially trained riot police from Glamorgan, nearly all of whom had already gained experience dealing with striking coal miners at Tonypandy. They were under the command of Supdt Williams, deputy chief constable of Glamorgan. Many arrived with bicycles and riot shields, while 'all were equipped for camping out'.[19] In the event many were billeted with local people, increasing the animosity. They were supported by 60 police from Bristol and 30 from Devonport, Plymouth.

They didn't have to wait long for trouble to occur at a number of places in the clay district. On 5 September there was an incident at Great Halbiggin [sic] works when the engine house was attacked with stones. The two policemen guarding the engine man – one Welsh, one local – were then attacked with sticks when they came outside. They retaliated with their batons.[20] The vociferous Baptist minister, Revd Booth

St Austell Constabulary, c.1913. Nearly every one of these well-built police officers sports a moustache. The photograph includes: Inspector Ernest Hugo (front row, centre) *and a sergeant wearing South African campaign medals* (front row, seventh from left). (MR P. CLEMO)

Coventry, was reported as commenting that 'the bringing in of these Welsh policemen was the most disastrous step that the officials could have taken'.[21]

He might well have been right, for there was a serious fracas near Bugle when a body of strikers was dispersed by the police. Two wagonette loads of women pickets had turned up from St Austell, organised by Miss Varley, an organiser of industrial action from the Black Country. They were in good humour when they arrived at Bugle; however, as the crowd swelled around the local clay works, the police urged the onlookers to disperse. Mr Vincent and Miss Varley began to protest against the intervention by the police. There was a scuffle, then, as one eyewitness recorded:

At this point the Glamorgans took the law into their own hands. Immediately, the order was given to charge... and before the onlookers or the crowd could realise what was happening Mr Vincent was pushed back into the forefront of the crowd... Batons were out quick as lightning, and as they descended with great force upon their heads the crowd was dumbfounded. 'Crack! Crack! Crack!' with startling quickness the batons fell upon the heads of the nearest.[22]

By the following week a number of works had reopened and many men had gone back to work.

The focus of attention now turned to the transshipping of clay. When 17 wagons of clay were sent to Charlestown under police escort they met with increasing hostility. As they moved down the hill through Tregonissey an attempt was made to interfere with the delivery and one poor wagon driver had a foot crushed under a wheel. When they arrived at the port the police officers were subjected to stone throwing. 'PC Hawken was struck on the thigh with a stone. PC Stapleton complained of being hit on the arm, and PC Pack, of the Devons, on the leg'.[23] The police were forced to draw their batons

and charge at the crowd, who duly dispersed.

Meanwhile, despite all the trouble, the employees had remained resolute. While the unions paid the strikers 10s. a week, men who were not members had struggled to survive with no income and by this time many were virtually destitute. Nor did they have the stomachs for an escalation in violence. The unions tried in vain to play down the growing perfidy, but it was to no avail; by 2 October some 85 per cent of the workforce had returned to work. Resumption of clay shipments began when 360 tons were loaded onto the *Activ*, docked at Charlestown. By 5 October the strike was over. It had gained nothing.

When the First World War started some ten months later, many clay workers left the industry, finding employment outside the county, either as soldiers or working in munitions industries. It is ironic that this led to a labour shortage which resulted in the granting of all the demands of 1913. A report on china clay workers' wages in August 1918 stated:

An agreement has been come to by the National Council of the China Clay Industry, representative of employers and workmen, for an increase of wages to meet war

The number of people emigrating from the area had passed its peak by the time this advertisement appeared in 1894, but the opportunity was still being promoted. (MR R. POAD)

THE CLAY STRIKE

STRIKE OUT FOR

DANIEL & ROWSE'S

SHIPPING OFFICES, ST. AUSTELL,

And Book your Passage to America, Canada,
or any Part of the World, where you CAN
earn good wages.

Book at once. Don't delay.

Papers, Pamphlets, and Sailings Free.

*The clay strike might have led to emigration from the area.
(Cornish Guardian, 29 August 1913, p.1.)*

conditions, in response to an application from the
Workers' Union to the Clay Employers' Federation for
50s. per week to day workers 18 and over.[24]

In fact wages reached a remarkable 63s. a week for a
short period in 1919. The war also was to bring about
dramatic social change. In 1918 all the china clay
employers recognised the unions, and there were
substantial pay rises over the pre-war rate.

In 1972 the BBC made a television drama of the
china clay workers' strike entitled *Stocker's Copper*. It
featured Bryan Marshall as Manuel Stocker, one of
the strikers, Jane Lapotaire as his wife Alice, and
Gareth Thomas as Herbert Griffith, a Welsh
policeman who was billeted with them. Some of the
opening scenes were filmed at a farm at Trezaise near
Roche where a china clay tip formed a suitable backdrop to a model railway laid out in a field on which
the steam engine was dramatically derailed – even if
this event was not historically correct. Since then this
significant episode in local history has, by and large,
fallen into obscurity.

*The filming of 'Stocker's Copper' by the BBC at a farm at
Trezaise near Roche in 1971. A model railway has been set
up on top of a wooden frame above a field hedge, while a
'tree' has been secured in the foreground.* (Mr R. Ridge)

Relations with the Local Community

The industry suffered from the national malady of
industrial action again during the 1970s. Yet despite
such unrest, the clay industry has generally enjoyed

a good relationship with its employees and the local
community. English China Clays International
(ECC) has long supported local community activities
such as sports events, choirs and bands. Houses
were built for employees and many people enjoyed
long years of service.

Health and Safety

Over the years there have been regular reports in the
local newspapers of injuries and deaths in the china
clay industry. Fortunately, in recent times safety has
taken a greater priority. In July 2004 Imery's Trebal
refinery celebrated 1,000 days without any 'lost-time
injury accident' (absence from work through injury),
and later won a prestigious gold award from the
Royal Society for the Prevention of Accidents
following the submission of a report showing three
years of continuous safety improvements.

References
[1] Kenneth Hudson, *The History of English China Clays
 – Fifty years of Pioneering Growth*, p.95.
[2] Ivor Bowditch, *The Essential Component*, p.6.
[3] Hudson, *op. cit*, p.160.
[4] Imerys Minerals Ltd, *Blueprint for Cornwall*, p.2, 10.
[5] *Ibid.*, p.10.
[6] *Ibid.*, p.8.
[7] *Cornish Guardian*, 21 February 1913, p.2.
[8] *Cornish Guardian*, 9 May 1913, p.6.
[9] *Cornish Guardian*, 20 June 1913, p.2.
[10] *Ibid.*
[11] *Cornish Guardian*, 27 June 1913, p.2.
[12] *Cornish Guardian*, 4 July 1913, p.5.
[13] *Royal Cornwall Gazette* 24 July 1913, p.5.
[14] *Cornish Guardian*, 25 July 1913, p.2.
[15] *Ibid.*
[16] *Royal Cornwall Gazette*, 31 July 1913, p.5.
[17] *Royal Cornwall Gazette*, 14 August 1913.
[18] *Ibid.*
[19] *Cornish Guardian*, 5 September 1913, p.2.
[20] *Cornish Guardian*, 5 September 1913, p.5.
[21] *Cornish Guardian*, 5 September 1913, p 7.
[22] *Ibid.*
[23] *Cornish Guardian*, 19 September 1913, p.2.
[24] *Royal Cornwall Gazette*, 28 August 1918, p.2.

Clay company terraced houses, Goverseth, 1920s.

(Wheal Martyn China Clay Museum)

Chapter 5

Outside the Town

Sandy Hill

Certain districts of St Austell, now commonly regarded as being part of the town, were once rural or suburban in nature. A good example of this is Sandy Hill, which descends from Polkyth to what was known as Sandy Bottom. Until Sandy Primary School was built in the 1970s, and Fairfield housing estate to the north, this was Sandy Farm. To the south, the area dubbed 'The Bird Sanctuary' (Chough Crescent, Gannet Drive, Kingfisher Drive and Cormorant Drive) was also built on open farmland at the same time. The decision to expand the town in this way was made by the council in the early 1960s, as revealed by the following newspaper statement:

Another far-reaching proposal, and indicative of the way the Council anticipates the town to grow, is that five areas of land should be included in the map [of the County Development Plan] for residential purposes.

The areas are at Gover Road; south of Sandy Hill from Daniels Lane to Slades Road; Belmont Road, St Austell; Tregonissey, St Austell; and Vernon Villas, St Blazey Gate.[1]

Over the years Sandy Hill itself has been both widened and straightened; pavements and more and more 'street furniture' have also been added to increase its urbanisation. The photographs clearly show the changing nature of this thoroughfare.

Haymaking at Sandy Farm, c.1935. Left to right, back row: *Tommy Hancock, ?, Bettie Hancock, Mrs Hancock*; middle row: *Tommy Stone, ?, Garnet Stone, ?, Ern Johns*; front row: *Leonard Hancock*.

Sandy Bottom

The Ordnance Survey map of 1888–1889 shows Sandy Bottom as a hamlet with cottages on either side of the road, and surrounded by a patchwork of

Sandy Bottom, c.1900. The road was little more than a lane with a gully at the side. (MR D. STONE)

Sandy Hill, 1907. There was still no pavement. Two cottages were then on the left-hand side, and the Carlyon Arms at the bottom of the hill. (MR M. STONE)

Electricity was installed in 1937. A pig shed is below the first cottage, and a cobbler's shop just up from the Carlyon Arms.

J. Nancarrow, carpenter, joiner and undertaker, photographed with his family outside his premises in Clifden Road, c.1905. The 'ope way' remains in 2005, as does the row of cottages, although the fronts have since been rendered.　(MRS B. WEBBER)

small fields. At the crossroads at the top of the hill, a school is shown where the council-houses stand in 2005. Polkyth was separated from the town by open fields stretching as far north as Tregonissey and south to Watering Hill which linked Mount Charles with the town.

Phernyssick

From Sandy Bottom a footpath led gently up the valley, over a ford, and on to Phernyssick, past what was a hive of industry. Delightful cottages nestled in a sylvan setting, yet in harmony with a neighbouring clay dry, settling tanks and leats. Further north was machinery from previous mining ventures, including ore stamps (machinery used to separate the ore from the waste rock) and a water-wheel. An engine house is shown next to Phernyssick Road on the 1908 Ordnance Survey map.

Mount Charles

Clifden Road leads from the top of Sandy Hill to Mount Charles. Formerly known as Union Road, its appearance has changed dramatically over the years. It was listed under the village of Mount Charles in Kelly's *Directory of Cornwall* of 1935, and at that time

was the site of many small businesses. These included two painters and decorators, a radio dealer, cobbler, tailor, baker, and a grocer's and fruiterer. At that time it was the site of the offices of St Austell Rovers Football Club, as well as Mount Charles Working Men's Institute which is still there in 2005. Also on Clifden Road was Bridge (United Methodist) Chapel and the Primitive Methodist Chapel. Bridge Chapel was demolished during the 1980s, as was a row of cottages behind it, to make way for new housing. As a result, only sections of the original street scene remain. The former Primitive Methodist Chapel is a carpet warehouse in 2005, while one of the finest buildings in the road survives as Fernley's fish and chip shop. Leading off Clifden Road, Ranelagh Road was the address of several sea captains, no doubt operating out of the nearby port of Charlestown.

Charlestown

Descending from Mount Charles down one of the widest streets of any community in the county, one finds a village that appears, at least from a superficial glance, hardly changed since the nineteenth century. The story of how the harbour and village were constructed by Charles Rashleigh at the end of the eighteenth century is recounted on page 74. The village named in his honour remained in private hands until the mid-1980s, and the fact that residents rented their property from the estate ensured that it remained little changed. Occasionally cottages were improved or updated, and somewhat grudgingly, modern developments were adopted. For example, in 1913 a meeting of ratepayers, with E.J. Hancock presiding, was held to discuss lighting at Charlestown when it was 'recommended that sixteen lamps should be fixed in the neighbourhood'. Mr H.E. Riley, manager of St Austell Gas Company, said that more should be added each year. They also discussed having a seat on the cliffs above the village.[2]

The United Methodist church (Bridge Chapel) in Clifden Road in 1975. By then it also served as a youth and community centre, but was beginning to look run down.

(MRS B. WEBBER)

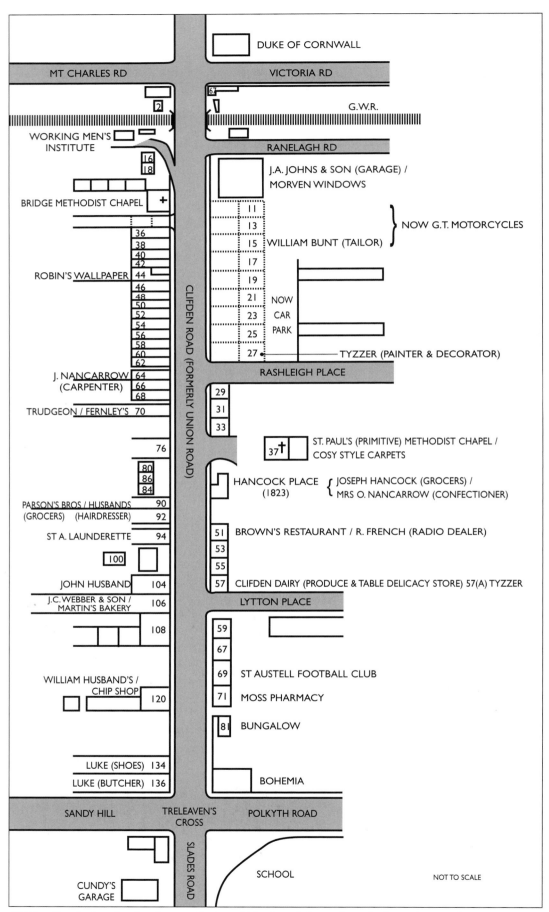

Clifden Road, showing businesses that could be found there since the late-nineteenth century.

The back of Bridge Chapel, Clifden Road, and a row of neighbouring cottages that were clearly in a parlous state and ready for demolition judging from the irregular line of the lintels. (Mr R. Dutch)

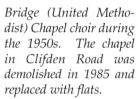

Bridge (United Methodist) Chapel choir during the 1950s. The chapel in Clifden Road was demolished in 1985 and replaced with flats.

(Mrs B. Webber)

Hancock Place in Clifden Road. The original part of the building was constructed in 1823. It is seen here on 15 August 2003 following a fire, and has since been renovated.

Some change has been inevitable in recent years. The harbour, which used to cater for the import of commodities such as coal and the export of china clay, has become home to square-rigged sailing vessels which serve the film industry. Several films have benefited from scenes filmed in the village itself. These have included the screen version of *The Day of the Triffids*, *Darwin's Voyage of Discovery*, *The Three Musketeers*, and the television drama *A Respectable Trade*. One of the biggest productions was the film adaptation of Jack Higgins's wartime drama, *The Eagle Has Landed*. In 1976 Charlestown was chosen to represent a port in the occupied Channel Islands because it had changed so little. Many locals were extras, which, as it turned out, involved much sitting round in anticipation and little glamour. A black-and-red striped sentry box was constructed next to the harbour where an MTB (motor torpedo boat) was berthed, and a machine-gun nest of sandbags was placed on the pier. In fact, sandbags seemed to be everywhere! In one memorable scene someone was thrown through the sandbag-protected window of the Pier House Hotel.

Ironically, some 36 years earlier the Home Guard

G. J. Larcombe
Monumental
Sculptor = =

Monuments, Headstones,
Crosses, Tablets, Vases,
In Marble, Granite & Slate.

Re-Lettering, Repairs, and
Renovations in Town or
Country.

Estimates and Designs.

THE FIRS,
MOUNT CHARLES,
ST. AUSTELL.

Larcombe, Mount Charles. In 2005 the firm continues to trade from the same premises as Kenross, although the crane that once stood outside has gone (from Harding's Guide Map to the District of St Austell, *c.1920s).*

had been watching from the roof of the Cornish Riviera Lido Club, only a short distance away, for a real German invasion. The club had been built during the 1930s, along with tennis-courts, a beach café and a swimming-pool. Indoor tennis had also been available, as well as billiards, snooker, squash and badminton. The dance floor was often the focus of regular black-tie dinner dances on Saturday nights. These events continued into the 'Swinging Sixties'. In 1964 *Old Tyme Music Hall* was being staged. Other popular forms of entertainment there were bathing beauty competitions, including the Miss South Coast competition, and wrestling, when the establishment was under the control of the enterprising and popular managers, Bill and Mabel Tull. Acts which performed at the club included The Temperance Seven, Acker Bilk, Kenny Ball, Sid Phillips and Chris Barber, as well as the resident local group, Cousin Jacks.[3]

During the 1970s the complex also housed 'Bentleys' disco, the black walls of which disappeared when the establishment was completely revamped in 1985; it reopened as 'Quasars', under the slogan 'The Nightspot for the Nineties'. With

Charlestown, 15 July 1994.

With echoes of former times, a busy Charlestown Harbour is seen on 1 September 1994, with a clay ship being loaded ahead of the square-sailed ships. This was one of the last shipments of clay from the port.

Charlestown Harbour became a film set for the BBC's A Respectable Trade *on 18 May 1997. Fake façades of buildings are being constructed on the quay for this story about the slave trade. Of course, in reality Charlestown played no part in this.*

The making of The Three Musketeers *at Charlestown, 17 July 1993.*

A view of Charlestown Harbour, c.1950. It makes an interesting comparison with the photogragh on page 75 as the first buildings have appeared on the skyline at Carlyon Bay to the north of Appletree Mine. Gas lamps can still be seen around the harbour. The cottage on the left was the abode of the harbour master, while to its right is the former 'Content' pilchard cellar.

Loading china clay at Charlestown during the summer of 1991. The hatches of the bulk carrier have been drawn back, allowing the chute to deliver the cargo into the hold. Clouds of dust from the china clay would shroud the harbourside and cottages, while the glare from the whitened quay dazzled pedestrians.

The demolition of Charlestown Garage, 22 December 2002. The roofless workshops can be seen behind the wall. The site was used to create West Polmear Court. The chapel is on the right.

bright pink and grey decor, several floor levels, two bars, and lights that could be lowered over the dance floor, it was more sophisticated and proved very popular. For a time it was augmented by the more exclusive 'Ocean Suite' which overlooked the by-now decrepit swimming-pool.

During the 1980s, in an attempt to improve the acoustics in the main hall, a lower false ceiling was added, and the bar was elongated – although the service was no quicker. By now called the Coliseum, the club was host to a number of top performers including Chris de Burgh, Duran Duran, Black Sabbath and Blondie. The large sign on the front of the building proudly informed the public of forth-coming events. Jazz was also popular, and jazz drummer Buddy Rich and his orchestra, as well as Johnny Dankworth, played there.

In 1990 Paul Higgins was brought in to run the Coliseum. Names such as Paul McCartney, Cliff Richard, Shirley Bassey and Alice Cooper lit up the large advertising hoarding. The Coliseum was also the venue for other popular events, regularly hosting the Radio One Roadshow each summer, as well as 'State' trade fairs, motor shows, the F3 Powerboat Championship and firework displays.

During the late-twentieth century Polgaver Beach gained notoriety from being designated a nudist beach.

Higher and Lower Porthpean

Further west along the coast were two distinct villages, Higher and Lower Porthpean. At the top of the hill that runs between them sits the church of St Leven and a scattering of

The catalogue of St Austell's 1965 trade fair, held at the Cornish Riviera Lido. It boasted that: 'the most modern and up-to-date Town Centre Development scheme in the South West has been started and is rapidly taking shape. This is a project of which St Austell can be justly proud and is a symbol of the forward-thinking and energy of the indus-trialists and traders of the area'. Sadly, the new town centre failed to live up to these aspirations. (MR R. DUTCH)

A view of the 1966 St Austell trade fair that took place in the Hall at Carlyon Bay, with closely-packed stands of local businesses. Sadly, Hickling Electrical and the Co-op appear to be the only ones in the picture that still survive in 2005 (ECC Ltd now being part of the French-owned Imerys Minerals Ltd).

(MR R. DUTCH)

houses and farm buildings. Along with Pentewan church, it is run by the clergy of St Austell. A row of fishermen's cottages once stood at the bottom opposite the modern-day car park, whilst a pilchard cellar overlooked the beach where the sailing club operates in 2005.

For many years the beach was popular with local families. There was a stall there that sold chocolates, sweets and fruit, as well as providing boiling water for making pots of tea. A similar service was provided by Mrs Brenton from her cottage above the beach. Benches and tables were set out amongst the apple trees where people could eat their pasties and sandwiches, and enjoy a cup of tea, before going down to the beach. At the bottom of the slipway was a boathouse run by the Axford brothers who for many years hired out deck-chairs and rowing boats.

Trenarren

On the other side of Black Head is the hamlet of Trenarren. Hidden amongst the tall, dark pines frequented by cackling rooks is Trenarren House, the former home of the late Dr A.L. Rowse, the eminent author, poet and historian who was born at Tregonissey in 1903. Beyond the white-painted cottages a twisty path leads to Hallane. The cottage above the little beach was once a water-mill, but survives as a seasonal holiday let in 2005.

Par, St Blazey and Tywardreath

It is hard to believe that on the eastern side of St Austell Bay, the sea once came inland as far as St Blazey: it is said to have lapped the walls of the churchyard. The community once boasted a foundry,

the Aberdeen laundry, and a fine Town Hall that later became the Palace cinema, then the Rainbow Rooms club during the 1970s and 1980s, and has now been turned into apartments.

The fields below Tywardreath church also rolled down to the marshy estuary. After it silted up, this area became Par Green – the name 'Par' actually means 'swamp'. Tywardreath Priory was the subject of Henry VIII's critical survey *Valor Ecclesiasticus* in 1538 and when, as a result of its findings, the monasteries were dissolved, the manor of St Austell was annexed from it, though the priory itself survived until the following reign of Edward VI. By then its few occupants had fallen into disrepute. The building was soon broken up, and the valuable stone incorporated into the nearby church and other buildings so that today no evidence of this, St Austell's former mother church, survives.

Clay Villages

Of all the communities in the St Austell district the clay villages are the ones that resisted change the most during the 1990s. Certainly places such as Whitemoor, Nanpean, Bugle and Roche have seen a significant increase in population during the 1990s, and a corresponding growth of new houses. Yet, situated amidst the debris of the local extraction industry, they have managed to retain their unique character, and their residents have retained their indomitable spirit and sense of community.

References
[1] *Cornish Guardian*, 26 January 1961, p.8.
[2] The *Royal Cornwall Gazette*, 15 May 1913, p.2.
[3] Peter Hancock, *St Austell – The Golden Years*.

Porthpean, c.1890.

Chapter 6

Transport

Roads and Mapping

The western approach to the town was originally via the turnpike road leading to the narrow little granite bridge over the St Austell River (also known as the White River) at Pondhu. Built in the sixteenth century, it led up the precipitous 'Old Hill' or West Hill to Fore Street. Although still standing in 2005, the bridge was closed to vehicles during the 1990s.

In 1675 Britannia, one of the first road atlases of England and Wales, was published by John Ogilby. It contained strip road maps, drawn as if along ribbons of paper, and showed the main roads from London to Land's End, including the junctions leading off it, as well as hills and spot heights. East of 'Grampond' there are junctions to 'Mowan' (St Mewan), before the road traverses high land. The road then crosses St Austell River (which was not named on the map), and spurs lead off to 'Trewrick', 'Tregorick', 'Penrise', 'Polemeer' (later Charlestown), Mevagissey and 'Polemeer' (East Polmear near Par). 'St Austle' is marked by a row of red terraced houses on either side of the road, as well as the church positioned in the region of the right-hand border. Interestingly, Ogilby's route passes a red post-mill (a windmill built on a central post) before entering 'Foy'. The base of a stone tower mill survives to this day at Windmill, Fowey.

It has to be remembered that in modern times this road would be regarded as little more than a narrow, unpaved track. Few, apart from merchants, attempted to travel any great distance, and progress would have been slow and difficult, particularly in the winter months.

Change came about slowly. Truro Road was constructed during the 1830s, forming an easier route into the town than West Hill. At the time this broad, relatively level and direct route must have been seen as a vast improvement, and soon large dwelling-houses were built next to the road. The modern Bodmin Road dates from around 1840.

With the completion of the railway link in 1859 new access roads to the station were constructed at Palace Road and later King's Avenue, again lined by fine houses. St Austell's bypass was created in 1926, including a new bridge over the White River, and is still dated 1926, although it was subsequently widened.

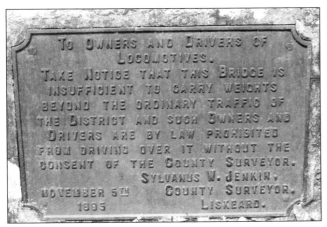

A warning sign of the weight limit on the approach to the sixteenth-century bridge which spans the St Austell River, dated 1895. In the late 1990s the bridge was closed to all but pedestrians on similar grounds.

An eighteenth-century painting of the old bridge at the bottom of West Hill, which provided the original access to the town. Topographically inaccurate, this somewhat fanciful view shows a rather wide St Austell River; it is hard to imagine it was ever broad enough at this point to enable the men to enjoy angling. (Mr R. Dutch)

A stagecoach such as this one, photographed in about 1900, would make regular trips, stopping at coaching inns along the way. (Mr R. Dutch)

71

West Hill, 1960.

Looking west along Truro Road. There is little traffic, although evidence of past travellers lies in the road.

(Mr W. Pappin)

Old buildings that once stood in Globe Yard, Truro Road, adjoining the Public Rooms, c.1962. These included the premises of tobacconist, S. Truscott. (Mr R. Dutch)

Church Street, c.1900.

Street Names

Within the town itself the origins of most of the street names are obvious, such as Truro Road, Bodmin Road, East Hill and Church Street. The exceptions may be High Cross Street, which was probably named after a churchyard cross that might have stood where The Red Bank is situated at the time of writing. Duke Street gained its name from a duck pond that is said to have been situated on the site of the Royal British Legion Club. Biddick's Court, once known as 'Biddick's Ope', leading off Fore Street, is named after a Dr Biddick who had the curious habit of visiting his patients after dark. Trinity Street, linking South Street, Bodmin Road and Truro Road, was a more recent addition, created in 1962.

Transporting Clay

Due to the state of the roads and the insular nature of most of the population, it was not until the arrival of the railways during the nineteenth century that many would have contemplated a long journey. Even then, passenger transport was low on the list of priorities. Large quantities of raw materials were, however, transported by road.

Much of the clay from the mines was carried by horse and wagon, the cargo either carried loose, in blocks (known as 'ball clay'), in bags, or 5cwt or half-ton casks, some of which were made at the cooperage at Charlestown using barrel staves imported from the Baltic. ECC Ltd maintained cooperages at Drinnick, Burngullow and Lee Moor. The clay was brought down Bodmin Road, through Fore Street and up East Hill. Here the horses were allowed to slake their thirst in the metropolitan drinking trough[1] that was opposite the site of Cooksley's the butcher in 2005, or in the stream at the side of Alexandra Road (then known as Watering Hill). The clay was then carried through Mount Charles and on towards Charlestown. In the early 1800s about 30 to 40 wagons a day were using Charlestown Road to reach the harbour. Each wagon could transport three to four tons of clay and teams of two to four horses were needed to climb the steep gradients.

By the 1900s road transport had been reduced as the railways took more clay and producers began to pipe liquid clay to 'dries' close to the harbours at Charlestown and Par. The last horse-drawn load was taken to the harbour in July 1949.

The Development of Charlestown

Charlestown Harbour was constructed between 1791 and 1800. Originally, shipping clay and ore from West Polmear (or Porthmear) involved beaching the vessels so that they could be loaded; this was an irregular and hazardous affair. It was Charles Rashleigh, the local landowner, lawyer and businessman who came up with the idea of creating a harbour, complete with a pier wall to shelter vessels. Exploiting a natural cleft in the cliff, thousands of tons of rock were excavated by hand to create the inner basin. Rashleigh also had the foresight to provide a leat that brought water to the harbour so that a satisfactory level could be maintained, and to enable the harbour to be flushed out (see Chapter 7) as well as creating a cliff battery to defend his investment.

Ancillary businesses quickly developed in the rapidly growing village, including more pilchard cellars, a shipyard at the head of the dock, limekilns, a cooperage and smithy, a rope-walk, as well as an inn and hotel. By 1830 there was a Wesleyan chapel and by 1851 a church. The village was later renamed after its founder by the grateful citizens. Over the years the dock was widened and loading facilities were improved. In 1971 the old harbour entrance was enlarged and the old wooden lock gates replaced by steel, horizontally hinged ones (still in place in 2005). Typically, china clay was exported, while ships brought in coal, timber and limestone.

The Pentewan Railway

Charlestown would not be without its rivals. To facilitate the export of china clay, as well as to bring in coal and other commodities, a narrow-gauge railway to Pentewan was constructed, opening in 1829. By then the harbour had been rebuilt by Sir Christopher Hawkins of Trewithen, near Probus, while a terminus was created at the foot of West Hill. The track, nearly 6.5km long, followed the St Austell River (known locally as the White River) through the Pentewan Valley, while the wagons relied on gravity and horses to ply their trade. Locomotives were not introduced until 1874, first using an 0-6-0 tender engine named 'Pentewan', followed by 'Trewithen' in 1886 and 'Canopus' in 1901. From 1912 she was supplemented by 'Pioneer', a 2-6-2 ST.

Although built to compete with the harbours at

A clay wagon ascending East Hill, c.1920s. They are just passing a drinking trough where the horses were able to have a well-earned drink before continuing down Watering Hill, through Mount Charles and on to Charlestown. (MR W. PAPPIN)

Charlestown Harbour, 1930s. The skyline at Carlyon Bay is free of housing, and the old engine house at Appletree Mine can be seen, the name deriving from an orchard in the vicinity run by some monks.

Charlestown and Fowey, throughout its life Pentewan had the disadvantage of suffering from silting, either from sand washed down from the clay works or swept in by storms at sea. Tanks were constructed to the north-west of the harbour – and subsequently enlarged – to provide reservoirs of water to flush out the basin, but these largely proved ineffectual.

In 1842 J.T. Treffry developed the harbour at Par, linking it with the clay works via a canal and railway to Bugle. Meanwhile proposals were put forward to extend the Pentewan Railway westwards to St Stephen or northwards up the Trenance Valley to the clay pits at Higher Ninestones, Gunheath, Goonbarrow, Wheal Martyn and Carthew. However, this never happened. A rival broad-gauge scheme, the Cornwall Railway, won the day when they secured an Act of Parliament in 1846. The railway passed through the town on its route between Truro and Saltash – and beyond, once Brunel's Royal Albert Bridge was completed in 1859. However, the important Trenance branch line did not exist until May 1920.

Another scheme to extend the Pentewan Railway was mooted in 1874 and again in 1886, this time

Duporth Manor, the home of Charles Rashleigh from 1779 to 1823. The house was demolished in 1988.

(HERITAGE & SHIPWRECK CENTRE, CHARLESTOWN)

The gardens of Duporth Manor, 1930. The message on the back of this postcard describes it as a beautiful place.

Charlestown Harbour, c.1890.

Charlestown Harbour, 1960s.

The plaque on the side of Pentewan Harbour, dated 1826.

historian, Dr A.L. Rowse, had fond memories of travelling to Pentewan and back on one such outing:

... the excitement was increased a hundredfold by the fact that we went down the valley, not by road, but by the diminutive railway that carried china clay to the harbour and coal back to the town. The trucks were cleaned out for this annual event, and filled with Sunday School forms... we couldn't have been more excited and tingling with expectancy if we were making a journey into Darkest Africa. And actually when we left the obviousness of the roadway behind us and the track took us beside the river skirting King's Wood, the river might have been the Limpopo and the wood equatorial forest, it was all so exotic and thrilling.[2]

Soon, however, the transportation of clay by rail began to decline and was balanced out by an increase

Trenance Viaduct, as a trestle bridge, looking from the Brake towards the town, 1890s. The pillars are, surprisingly, hollow. (MRS J. WILCOCKS)

using an electrified central rail on a revised gauge of 3ft. Despite high hopes and influential backers, this was never achieved.

Passenger Transport

Prior to 1883, little consideration had been given to carrying passengers, but then the Pentewan Railway began to offer free Sunday-school excursions, something which was to prove popular with many. The

Old railway sheds at West Hill that once formed part of the Pentewan Railway. (MR R. SANDERCOCK)

in transportation of sand and other cargoes. Despite this, the end of the line came during the First World War. Clay production fell, and exports via Par, Fowey and Charlestown were proving more efficient. A government 'request' for the engines, rolling stock and track for the war effort finished it off.

The Great Western Railway

Meanwhile the Great Western Railway had prospered. During the 1890s the old wooden trestle viaducts, like those at Trenance, were replaced by stone arches. In 1892 the line itself was swiftly

A wonderful early view of St Austell Station, pre-dating the erection of the footbridge in 1882. A ladder rests against the water-tower, while pens for animals and casks are on the right below Palace Road. The substantial hedge is long gone. (MR R. DUTCH)

Locomotive 7925 'Westol Hall', leaving St Austell Station at 1.30.p.m., 3 August 1956. (MRS J. WILCOCKS)

converted from broad gauge to narrow gauge. A goods' depot was built at St Austell Station, to the north of the track, followed by a substantial building in the station yard. The retaining wall of the station yard was built of granite blocks of impressive proportions, similar to the new viaducts. Later, a third goods' depot was created at Polkyth, opening on 2 November 1931. The depot finally stopped taking general goods in May 1968, although it was used on and off until 1985. In 2003 the site was cleared to make way for an 'urban village' inspired

This bus was purchased by the GWR in 1908.
(MR A. DELLER)

A GWR bus on its way to St Dennis, c.1925.
(MR W. PAPPIN)

A GWR bus photographed in April 1913. T. Williams & Son, family butcher and game dealer in Fore Street, are advertised on the side of the open top deck. (MR R. DUTCH)

The original Trenance Viaduct.

by Prince Charles's vision at Poundbury in Dorset.

St Austell Station was equipped with platforms, station buildings and a water-tower. Until 1931 Trevarthian Road crossed the line at a level crossing, but was then replaced by a footbridge. The elegant footbridge between platforms was constructed in 1882 and has survived subsequent changes. Stationmasters at St Austell over the years included Messrs Sylvester, Davey, Trewine and Henwood. GWR buses ran from the station to outlying districts.

Railway sheds at St Blazey provided maintenance facilities, with both cleaning shops for servicing boilers, furnaces etc., and fitting shops for mechanical repairs. From here Squire Treffry's previous Cornwall Mineral Railway ran via Luxulyan to Bugle. The line had opened in 1870, and in 1874 commenced carrying passengers; in the same year it was extended to Newquay. On 1 October 1877 the GWR took it over. In 1893 a branch line was opened from Bugle to Goonbarrow, providing access to the clay works which had for so long been denied the Pentewan Railway.

GWR locomotive 6911 'Holker Hall' leaving St Blazey railway sheds on 5 May 1957. (Mrs J. Wilcocks)

The railway line running through Bugle. This is part of the Goonbarrow branch line, showing the loop into Bean Dries. Charles Street and Bilberry clay works are in the background. (Mrs J. Wilcocks)

Luxulyan railway station in 1922. Note the water-tower and the windmill used for pumping water into the tanks to supply the engines.

(MRS J. WILCOCKS)

Bugle railway station in 1906, showing the old three-storey signal-box, replaced by GWR in 1913 at Molinnis Crossing. Advertisements adorn the railings, while casks of clay can be seen in the foreground.

(MRS J. WILCOCKS)

SINGER

NINE H.P. POPULAR SALOON
A ROOMY, COMFORTABLE FOUR DOOR,
HIGH EFFICIENCY SALOON FOR £162.10.0

Hand built body, aluminium panelled, on Ash frames, sliding roof, adjustable bucket seats, rear blind, glove boxes, ash tray, door pockets, every conceivable luxury fitting.

It can hum its effortless way through traffic, and travel all day long without fuss—without effort

The most remarkable value we have ever seen.

Come, see, and try it without obligation.

ST. AUSTELL. 'PHONE: 78.
'Grams: "IGNITION."

Singer cars were available from Hill & Phillips (advertised in the Cornish Guardian, *28 March 1935, p.4).*

The Cornwall Aviation Company

The story of this celebrated pioneering air service was centred around the charismatic young aviator, Percival Phillips. His illustrious and daredevil career began when, at the outbreak of the First World War, he joined the Devon and Cornwall Light Infantry, upon which he was promptly sent to serve in India. Then in August 1915 he volunteered for the Royal Flying Corps. This saw him transferred to Iraq where he first worked as a mechanic. However, after making his first flight in 1916 he was smitten and decided to train as a pilot. This was undertaken in Egypt, before he returned to his old unit in March 1918. He was soon the recipient of a DFC (Distinguished Flying Cross) for his bravery and prowess as an aviator.

On his return to St Austell in 1919 he became a partner in Hill & Phillips's Garage. He soon settled down and married a local girl, Lylie Pauline Rowse, although he remained in the RAF Reserve.

Following the overhaul of aircraft engines for the Berkshire Aviation Company, which took place at the garage in 1924, Phillips was inspired to form the Cornwall Aviation Company. His first aircraft, purchased from a customer, was an Avro 504K, which cost £250. It was registered G-EBIZ and flown from Rocky Park on the western outskirts of the town.

After providing joyrides at 5s. per passenger, in 1925 he went on a tour of the West Country. At this time flying was still very much a novelty for the general public, and his tour proved popular. As a result, in 1926 a second aircraft was acquired. This was another Avro, registered G-EBNR. Then in 1927 Avro G-EBSE was purchased, and additional pilots joined the company. As well as joyrides, stunts and aerobatics, the planes were also used to tow advertising banners, a sight that is still familiar in 2005. In 1929 G-EBIZ was converted into a four-seater, and another aircraft, Avro G-AAAF, was purchased. By 1931 the company had carried some 95,000 passengers. However, the work was seasonal and the pilots had to find other employment in the winter months while the aircraft were overhauled.

In 1932 the Cornwall Aviation Company teamed up with the famous Cobham's Flying Circus, operating as the National Aviation Day Display Campaign. The tour took in 170 different towns throughout the country. As a result of its success, the tour was repeated in subsequent years. Then in 1936 Phillips, along with C.W.A. Scott, took over Cobham's Flying Circus and renamed it C.W.A. Scott's Flying Display Ltd. However, following a long period of inclement weather that summer, accompanied by poor attendance, in September the company went into voluntary liquidation.

Undeterred, Phillips formed a new company, Air Publicity Ltd. This involved towing advertising banners on behalf of a wide range of firms throughout the country. For some time Heston had been the main centre of operations, while the offices were in London.

After towing one such banner, on Sunday 13 February 1938, Phillips called in on some friends in Cambridgeshire. After lunch he took off with his faithful dog, Kim. Tragically his plane crashed just after take off, when failing to clear a tree. Phillips died shortly after.

The following year Air Publicity Ltd pilots were absorbed into the war effort. We can only speculate on the role Phillips might have played in the conflict. However, by then the aircraft themselves were being regarded as antiques and had a limited role.

Plans for an Airport in St Austell

In May 1935 the St Austell chamber of commerce had been looking for a site for a town airport and sought Phillips's help. This had the backing of local hoteliers, but sadly the idea was never developed. It was stated in the *Cornish Guardian* of 30 May that:

At the meeting of St Austell Chamber of Commerce, on Monday night, Mr Charles Hodgson presiding, an interesting announcement was made of developments in the direction of the establishment of an airport in the St Austell area.

The Chairman announced that the Executive had been in touch with Capt. Percival Phillips, the St Austell airman, and had explored several possible sites for an aerodrome and he was glad to say they had found one [but] it was inadvisable to say where it was at the moment, but he could assure them that it was very convenient and Capt. Phillips told them that it would pass the Air Ministry tests.[3]

In all likelihood the site was at Rocky Park.

The plans never materialised. However, nearly 30 years later, in January 1961, a similar scheme was hatched to create a heliport at St Austell, and again a site was considered. It was reported in the *Cornish Guardian* that:

ST AUSTELL URBAN COUNCIL is to ask the County Planning Authority to earmark Rocky Park as a possible site for a Heliport when the Town Map of the County Development Plan is reviewed. Rocky Park is on high ground near Truro Road a mile from the town.[4]

Again the idea was never brought to fruition, so that today the nearest airport to the town is St Mawgan.

Local Garages

The most enduring form of transport, and the one that would have the greatest impact on the town, was the motor car. As well as Hill & Phillips's Garage, St Austell has been blessed with a large number of garages and service stations. From the 1920s to 1950s

Pugh's Garage was in Truro Road (from Harding's Guide Map to the District of St Austell, *c.1920s).*

Pugh's Garage (advertised in the Cornish Guardian, *11 July 1929, p.5).*

White Hart Garage (advertised in the Cornish Guardian, *30 April 1926, p.11).*

A wonderful shot of a special event, the Standard Triumph Service Week in East Hill Garage. The early Triumph Herald with a handle on the bonnet dates from 1959/60. An engine, gearbox and suspension units are on display, while posters on the wall advertise the Standard Vanguard and Triumph TR3 sports car. Even the dog is interested in one of the displays.

(MR R. DUTCH)

East Hill Garage, run by St Austell Garages Ltd, seen during the early 1960s, was neat and tidy, with flower tubs in front of the forecourt and a kiosk for the petrol attendant. (MR R. DUTCH)

Phillips & Geake Ltd had premises in Beech Road, to the rear of the Police Station. This photograph was taken in 1965, though the scene is little changed in 2005, apart from the absence of the petrol pumps, it being the American Car Centre. Phillips & Geake would take over Cundy's Garage at the bottom of Slades Road.

(MR R. DUTCH)

Pugh's Garage thrived in Truro Road, and the firm made use of the old Savoy cinema for servicing tractors. In 2005 part of their premises is used by St Austell Printing Co. Ltd. Assheton-Salton ran White Hart Garage in East Hill until 1945. During the Second World War they produced components needed for the war effort. St Austell Garages Ltd had premises in East Hill, the site of Vosper's Ford and Fiat agency in 2005. Phillips & Geake originally had a garage in Beech Road, but moved to larger premises at the foot of Slades Road during 1963. Meanwhile By-Pass Transport kept local garages supplied with new cars using their transporter.

References

1 A similar drinking trough can still be seen beside the bypass, to the west of the petrol station.
2 A.L. Rowse, *A Cornish Childhood*, p.139.
3 *Cornish Guardian*, 30 May 1935, p.13.
4 *Cornish Guardian*, 26 January 1961, p.8.

A car delivery service was provided by By-Pass Transport (St Austell) Ltd, seen here during the early 1960s with a consignment of new Minis. (Mr R. Dutch)

The same transporter at White Hart Garage, at the bottom of East Hill, during the early 1960s. The building in the background survives, even though the garage is no more. (Mr R. Dutch)

Chapter 7

Local Employment

For centuries St Austell's residents relied upon Cornwall's traditional industries of farming, fishing and mining. While many gained permanent and lifelong employment in the china clay industry, others often faced periods of unemployment as their job depended on the vagaries of the local economy, the seasons, or the weather. It was not uncommon to find people working in more than one area, such as helping with the harvest after a day's work in a clay pit, or maintaining a smallholding to help support their family.

Farming

For centuries St Austell was surrounded by smallholdings and relatively small farms, many of them no longer with us, having been swallowed up by new housing estates. Pigot's *Directory of Devon and Cornwall* for 1830 described the area around the town thus:

The southern part of the parish is a fine agricultural country, the land gently undulating and fertile, with some pleasant views; on the northern part is a great extent of common.[1]

This early directory went on to explain that Friday was market day, and that fairs were held on 'the first Thursday before Easter, Thursday in Whitsun week, and St Andrew's Day, principally for cattle and sheep'. Tuesdays became established as cattle-market day, and some of the animals sold were then driven up to Tregonissey abattoir. On occasions the gutter at the side of Slades Road ran red with blood.

Before the Royal Cornwall Show had a permanent venue at Wadebridge, the annual agricultural show would move around the county. St Austell hosted the event on seven occasions between 1859 and 1954.

The Ordnance Survey map of 1888–1889 shows a town considerably smaller in area than in the early-twenty-first century, and surrounded by a patchwork of small fields. Heading east out of the town, open countryside stretched out as far as Polkyth, while to the south there were fields as far as the railway line and Watering Hill. At this time Slades Road was flanked by open countryside as far as Tregonissey, while Tregonissey and Sandy Bottom were isolated small hamlets. Heading further east from here one would have encountered numerous old shafts and mine workings to 'Bold-venture' and beyond. Today, Sandy Farm, Phernyssick Farm, and various smallholdings at Tregonissey have disappeared, due to tightly packed rows of new houses spreading like a rash across the hillsides and down the valleys.

Trenowah Farm, Tregrehan, near St Austell, 1960s. Mr E.G. Brokenshire is driving the tractor, harvesting the first crop of maize to be grown in Cornwall, the seed having been imported from America. The farm has now been built over and a housing estate stands on this site.
(MR R. DUTCH)

87

The Pilchard Industry

For centuries fishing was practiced in many of the coves in St Austell Bay (known as Tywardreath Bay until the late-eighteenth century). Pilchard 'cellars' or 'palaces' were built close to the shore so the catch could be quickly and conveniently processed. There was one at Hallane, Ropehaven and Porthpean, while Charlestown boasted three – known as Rashleigh, Friends' Endeavour and Content. Built in about 1740, the latter was probably the first building to be constructed in the village of Charlestown – originally called West Porthmear. In 2005 the building still survives above the cliffs to the east of the harbour, now converted into a private residence. Holes remain in the side walls through which poles were once inserted to exert pressure on the casks of pilchards, thereby squeezing out the oil.

One of the largest 'palaces' was at Polkerris, above the beach. Constructed as early as Elizabethan times, this building also survives in 2005. A 'huer' or lookout would have been stationed on a promontory to spot the large shoals of pilchards and alert the waiting boats, although no huer's hut, such as the one at Newquay, can be found within the crescent of St Austell Bay. Summoned with the cry of 'Heva!', the whole community would have been involved in the landing and processing of the catch during the pilchard season, between late summer and autumn. The men would use their boats to surround the shoals with their nets, then pull them towards the beach. Once the shoals were in shallow water, everyone would help remove the fish, and carry them in baskets to the nearby cellar, where they were cured in salt.

By the nineteenth century pilchard fishing was in decline, as boats went further afield in search of the shoals, and consequently fewer large shoals moved inshore. In 1867 the village's last seine boats, the nets and 100 tonnes of unused salt were sold at auction in the General Elliot public house, bringing an end to a traditional local industry.

Polkerris appears to be little changed in 2005. However, the area facing the sea where the General Elliot once stood, a little way north of the extant Rashleigh Inn, as well as other cottages (which formerly occupied the site of the pub car park), were claimed by a storm. Although the chapel and the village school adjoining the pilchard palace still survive, they no longer function in the manner their builders intended. Similarly, the lifeboat station is a beach shop, while the cottage gardens that ran up the side of the valley in narrow strips are largely overgrown.

Despite the demise of the pilchards, they were not the only fish that were in demand. In 1903 'a splendid catch of fish' was reported in the *Cornish Guardian*:

On Wednesday the fishing boats from Charlestown harbour landed a huge catch of mackerel, one boat containing no less than 800 fish. Now that mackerel are fetching something like 7s. per cwt, it is expected the boats will clear a good bit over their large haul. The catch was made only a short distance out from the harbour.[2]

Mevagissey inner harbour, 1920s.

It was left to the fishermen at Mevagissey to go further afield in pursuit of their catches. After all, they had a bigger harbour, and the facilities ashore were larger and greater in number.

Lifeboats

Besides the red-and-white striped daymark on the Gribben, constructed by Trinity House in 1832, maritime safety within St Austell Bay was partly the responsibility of the lifeboat stationed at Polkerris. The first lifeboat was stationed there in 1859, and as William Rashleigh and his wife Catherine were the main benefactors, it was christened *The Catherine Rashleigh*. Rather surprisingly, it had been constructed in London, brought by the newly opened railway as far as Lostwithiel where it was launched, and then rowed to its new station in the village. By the time it was replaced in 1922 the Polkerris lifeboat had been launched 24 times and saved 52 lives.

The lifeboat *James Chisholm* was stationed at Mevagissey between 1897 and 1927. During those years 44 lives were saved. The boat was 37ft long and had no engine, relying instead upon oars and sails. In 1927 a motor lifeboat was stationed at Fowey that was able to cover the whole bay, and the *James Chisholm* was sold off for the princely sum of £20. Mevagissey lifeboat station closed in 1930; the building survives as an aquarium in 2005.

Mining in the St Austell Area

It is possible that tin streaming was practiced in the valley leading from Carclaze to Holmbush by the Phoenicians c.2000–1200BC; it was certainly practiced as early as the Bronze Age. The remains of old, possibly medieval, alluvial tin workings were found at Holmbush, during the development of the Tesco site in the 1990s. Seams of tin and copper lay in the area, these being particularly rich to the east of the town, and during the early-nineteenth century a thriving metalliferous mining industry developed. When describing the town in 1830 Pigot's *Directory of Devon and Cornwall* gave its principal mines as follows:

> the copper-mines of 'Wheal Pembroke' and 'East Crennis', [sic] the 'Polgooth' and 'Beam' tin-mines; and between the town and Lostwithiel are the extensive copper-workings of 'Lanescot' and 'Fowey' consolidated mines.[3]

Yet remarkably, for such a widespread and environmentally destructive activity, there is little evidence of it today.

Ventonwyn Mine
The engine house and stack to the north of Sticker on the A390 road to Truro stands as a beacon on the hillside marking the small Ventonwyn Mine.

The launching ceremony for the Mevagissey lifeboat James Chisholm *in 1897. The new vessel is emerging from the lifeboat house, while ladies in boaters and long skirts look on. In the background open ground can be seen between The Battery and the old cottages nestling around the inner harbour.*
(MEVAGISSEY MUSEUM)

Great Hewas Mine

No evidence remains of the large Great Hewas Mine to the east of the town. At one time some 264 people were employed there.[4]

Great Polgooth Mine

On the top of the hill above Polgooth, and surrounded by St Austell golf course, a surviving engine house marks the position of Great Polgooth Mine. Another engine house in the village has been converted for residential use. In 1797 this mine boasted 50 shafts and over 1,000 people were employed there, with no less luminaries than Matthew Boulton and James Watt as adventurers in the enterprise. Further down the valley were Wheal Virgin at London Apprentice and Happy Union at Pentewan, which were to combine as Pentuan [sic] Stream Mine. F.W.L. Stockdale, writing of his excursions in 1824, was impressed by these mines:

... the stranger will be greatly astonished at the busy operations of the miners, in one of the largest Tin Stream Works in the county, which adjoins the road about half way [between St Austell and Mevagissey].[5]

Fowey Consols

Fowey Consols produced nearly a quarter of a million tons of copper, then worth about £1.5 million. In 1840 a total of 1,792 people were employed there. As well as the usual facilities, the mine boasted dormitories for workers, a candle factory and a rope-walk.[6] The mine, owned by Joseph Thomas Treffry (previously called Austen) of Place House, Fowey, was partly the reason for the construction of Par Harbour between 1829 and 1840. Granite from Luxulyan quarry, as well as china clay, was also shipped from there, utilising two inclines and a three-mile-long canal from Pont's Mill.

Foundries and Blowing Houses

William West (1801–79), the engineer who had designed all the machinery for Fowey Consols, took up residence at Tredenham House, St Blazey. He established the Foundry and Engine Works at St Blazey in 1848. This became a major source of employment in the district, as well as providing the facilities for creating the diverse range of equipment needed by the mines in the county. Not that this was the only one: St Austell already boasted two foundries, as noted by Slater in 1852–53:

There are two extensive iron foundries, where the machinery for the mines is constructed – Mr John Hodge of the 'Saint Austell Iron Foundry,' and Messrs James Thomas & Co., Charlestown, are proprietors.[7]

The foundries were served by blowing houses which smelted the ore that had been raised to the surface. Slater also observed that, 'adjoining the western part of the town, are three very spacious Blowing Houses'.[8]

Par Stack

Near Par Harbour, below Par Consols, was a lead smelting works which included the 235ft-high Par Stack, built to carry away the toxic fumes, and once the tallest chimney in Cornwall. In 1907 it was damaged by a lightning strike, so it was deemed necessary to demolish it. The task was given to a London steeplejack, Mr W. Larkins, and carried out

Loading china clay at Par Harbour, early-twentieth century. (Mevagissey Museum)

An old Par brick, a product of the brickworks that stood near Par Harbour in the late-nineteenth century.

before a large crowd of onlookers, without any peripheral damage. The chimney had been constructed from bricks made at the nearby brickworks using mud dredged from the harbour.

Copper Mines at Crinnis

Some of the greatest copper mines in the area were at Crinnis which, for a time in the early-nineteenth century, threatened the dominance of deeper mines at Gwennap and Camborne. In the first four months of 1813 they dispatched some 3,792 tons of ore from Charlestown to the smelters in Swansea. North of the Crinnis mines was Pembroke Mine which was also very productive during the 1820s, being Cornwall's second largest copper producer after

Consolidated in Gwennap. Its neighbour, East Crinnis, which extended as far as Spit, would surpass it in 1826. Little evidence of this lucrative mining activity remains today, apart from verdant mounds amongst the trees at Par Moor.

Charlestown United Mines

Charlestown United Mines to the north of Holmbush has been built over with houses and light industrial units. Once Bucklers, Fatwork and Wheal Virtue were prosperous tin mines, and it was recorded that in 1838 a total of 431 men, 120 women and 263 children were employed there.[9] With the addition of Cuddra and Boscundle (later called Wheal Eliza) mines to the east, in 1863 the area was the third largest tin producer in the county. A year later 512 people were employed there, but ten years later they had ceased working.[10]

Such was the pattern of boom and bust that was imprinted on many of the mines in the area: often they flourished, struggled, were taken over, amalgamated and revitalised, only to be abandoned during hard times. Wheal Eliza Consols was the last to remain open, surviving until 1892, by which time five miles of underground tramroads had been laid because working within the grounds of Tregrehan estate was forbidden.

Carclaze Mine

Not all of the mines required shafts and galleries. Carclaze, to the north of St Austell, was the site of a huge, ancient opencast mine, that by the nineteenth

The huge opencast clay mine at Carclaze, 1820s.

century was a mile in circumference and some 150ft deep. It even had a subterranean canal which enabled the ore to be brought to the stamps and dressing floors by small flat-bottomed boats. Early on, deposits of china clay were treated as overburden and dumped. However, by the mid-nineteenth century Carclaze was producing more and more china clay, with both tin and clay being extracted together. By 1877 tin production had virtually finished.

Gover, Halviggan, Beam and Goonbarrow Mines

Gover Mine was also developed from an opencast mine, and was possibly the only mine using stamps operated below ground.[11] A total of 30 people were employed there in 1870. Nearby Halviggan was worked intermittently and with varying success for tin. Beam Mine and Goonbarrow were also originally tin mines, and ones in which conditions were particularly bad because the ground was so soft and damp, largely comprising of sand and liquid clay. In 1864 a parliamentary commission found that the miners at Beam Mine 'were all old men at the age of forty'.[12]

Most of these mines were later swallowed up by the china clay industry (see Chapter 4).

Consequences for Modern Times

The landscape has recovered remarkably well after such extensive mining operations which, besides the underground workings, required engine houses, dressing floors, stamps and large areas on which to dump infertile mine waste. It is, however, often necessary to have a mining search conducted when a new house is planned, yet the maps and records are often incomplete or inaccurate, particularly for the more ancient workings, or when speculative shafts were dug and later abandoned. It has not been unknown for a hole to suddenly open up, or for a structure to suffer from subsidence as a result of an unseen collapse deep below ground.

Unique or Redundant Local Occupations

The Leat Man

When Charlestown Harbour was built at the end of the eighteenth century, it was necessary to construct a system of leats that could maintain a supply of water so that the dock could be regularly flushed out to remove silt and other debris. This originally ran from Bowling Green, near Bugle, but subsequently started from the Luxulyan Valley. The leat man was responsible for maintaining this system. This involved patrolling the leat along its course, removing fallen trees and other debris, as well as breaking up dams built by children or repairing collapsed embankments undermined by rabbits or rats. It was a solitary and potentially dangerous job,

General shipping in Charlestown Harbour, c.1900.
(Shipwreck & Heritage Centre, Charlestown)

for two sections ran underground. Sluices and weirs had to be maintained, as well as wooden shuttering. The two large ponds on the western side of Charlestown that served as reservoirs also had to be dredged.

The leat is still as important today for the smooth running of the harbour, and until recently, the role was undertaken by Mr John Dove. Once a month he would patrol the whole eight miles of leat. The two ponds, well stocked with roach, perch and trout, also had to be maintained, although the old cleaning system, utilising a series of sluices, has not been used since the early 1980s. More of the river is now enclosed inside pipes, including a length that runs beneath the North East Distributor Road.

The Kettle-Boy

During the 1930s, a boy who left school at 14 and gained a job in the china clay industry, might have begun his career as a kettle-boy. Such was the role of Mr Les Lean when he went to work at Coxborrow clay works, run by Parkyn & Peters. His job was to boil the kettle and warm the pasties for 'crib' for each of the different shifts, taken in the 'lodge' or crib hut. First he would need to fetch water from the 'bottoms' (the bottom of the pit) where there would be a lovely fresh supply straight out of the stone lode (ore-bearing rock). As well as this he had to fetch coal from the engine house, where he might pause to watch the equipment bringing the 'skips' up the incline, or carry 'dubbers' (chisel-pointed picks used for breaking up the clay) back to the blacksmith's shop to be sharpened. Later, as he got older and gained strength and experience, he, along with many youngsters like him, progressed to other jobs and different pits.

The Errand Boy

In modern times, the path to retail management may well begin with a menial task like stacking shelves. However, before the advent of supermarkets, potential managers often started out as errand boys in the grocery trade.

Having cycled to work, his first task of the day would be to scrub the shop floor. If it was a rainy day the black and white tiles would then be covered with a thin layer of sawdust to prevent any customers slipping over. On a Monday, when there were few deliveries to make, he might be told to clean all the brass, balance scales and weights that were used in the shop store, as well as the brass hopper attached to the coffee grinding machine.

Deliveries to the shop came via rail to the goods' yard at Polkyth. The errand boy would be expected to help unload the Great Western wagons which delivered the bags of flour, sugar, rice, bales of bacon, crates of cheese, boxes of butter, lard, margarine, currants, sultanas, prunes, dates, etc.

It was generally during the latter part of the week when the errand boy, having cleaned his bike, would fill the large wicker basket with parcels and make his deliveries to customers at Trenance, Eastbourne, Mount Charles, Porthpean, Charlestown, Holmbush, Bethel, Boscoppa, Tregonissey, Slades and Polkyth. On Saturdays, separate loads would have to be taken to St Blazey, Par and Tywardreath.

Mr Roscoe Poad was an errand boy during the 1920s. He recalls returning to the shop at 4p.m. one wet Saturday, only to be told by the manager that there was a boat order to be delivered to Pentewan Dock, so he had to venture out again. By the end of the day he had cycled over 50 miles!

Should the errand boy be promoted to junior assistant, his wage would rise from 10s. to 14s. a week. He would then be entrusted with the task of weighing up goods, such as flour, sugar, cereals, dried fruits, dates and New Zealand Anchor butter.

The next rung of the ladder was shop assistant. This called for good mental arithmetic, as purchases had to be added up in the head. He would also be taught how to welcome the customer, how to dress the shop window and create displays, and would go out on rounds taking orders that would be delivered by a van or the errand boy.

If they proved proficient, the assistant might be trained for the provision department, when he could earn 20s. a week, or 22s. if he became a senior assistant or 'first hand'. By then he would be training for management, learning book-keeping and gaining experience by relieving managers in other branches when they took a holiday.

Once a manager, he might expect to earn £5 a week, for which he was responsible for the successful running of the shop, and was then answerable to the inspector for Cornwall.

The route described above was taken by Mr Poad, as he progressed in the grocery trade in St Austell. Since his retirement he has done sterling service for a number of charities, to date raising over £34,000, including £22,000 for Macmillan Cancer Relief. As well as undertaking charity walks, at the age of 88 he abseiled down the side of County Hall in Truro, gaining a place in the *Guinness Book Of Records*.

The Telegram Boy

Before the advent of the telephone – let alone e-mail – the quickest form of communication was the telegram. The electric telegraph enabled messages to be sent over long distances, and by the 1840s public telegram services had been established. Telegrams were delivered by telegram boys. During the 1930s four were employed in the office in High Cross Street. They ventured out on push bikes in all weathers to deliver the messages as they came in. Telegram boys were provided with a uniform, and a little round hat with a strap, as well as a waterproof cape and leggings for inclement weather. Mr Beswarick of St Austell undertook such work during the 1920s. He recalls the clay offices being some of his most frequent destinations, where he delivered messages for the clay captains. Regular trips would also include the outlying villages, such as Polgooth, Greensplatt and Nanpean. Starting as a temporary boy messenger at St Austell in 1927, Mr Beswarick advanced to postman messenger. He later moved to Plymouth, where he became a postman, but returned to St Austell to become the executive officer (or chief inspector) in St Austell Post Office between 1962 and 1973.

The Ironmonger

Hodges was established in Fore Street as early as 1830, a date that was displayed for all to see on the renowned copper kettle that hung above the entrance. Mr H. Faul Hodge ran the shop from 1912 until about 1946. Mr Jack Blake, who worked there from 1925 to 1939, recalls that they sold everything from a quarter-inch screw to a range for the kitchen. Customers could buy paraffin, turpentine, linseed oil, cutlery, fishing tackle, china, buckets and pans – the list goes on. The store was always kept well stocked. Besides the shop in Fore Street there was a plumber's shop at Biddick's Court where fireplaces were also stored. Deliveries were made throughout the area by horse and trap.

Mr S.N. Beswarick, dressed in the uniform of a telegram boy, 1927. He is wearing a belt with a pouch to hold the messages. (MR S.N. BESWARICK)

Telegram boys looking smart in their uniforms, 1927. Left to right: Roy Lawer, 'Johnny' Beswarick and Frank Roberts. (MR S.N. BESWARICK)

The telegram boys with their bicycles, 1927. Notice the rod-operated brakes and lack of gears or lights. (MR S.N. BESWARICK)

Hodge's ironmonger's at 11 Fore Street, 19 December 1931. Standing at the door are Mr Jack Blake, Mr Sid Wickett and Mr Alf Wilson. Note the copper kettle above the entrance dated 1830 and the wide range of goods on display. The famous copper kettle was removed when Smith & Treffry acquired the shop in 1947, and was taken to their premises at Par. Fittingly, Mr Hodge's son was later able to purchase it from them. (MR J. BLAKE)

The Chimney Sweep

Until the 1970s most buildings were heated by open fires or stoves fuelled by coal. This was transported by sea to our local ports. Ships arriving at Charlestown would often bring coal from South Wales which would be stored in a number of coal yards in the village from where it would be distributed. In 2005, these open spaces, cobbled with surplus ballast, serve as the main car park and the car park for the Rashleigh Arms; only coal merchants R.A. Hawke & Sons retain a yard there.

In order for chimneys to work efficiently and to avoid any build-up of soot which could then catch fire, chimney sweeps were kept busy. One family that served the local community was the Metters of St Tudy. Widowed early, Mrs Metters brought her sons into the business and they have now been established since the 1950s, cleaning the chimneys of private houses not only in mid-Cornwall but to the north and east of the county, as well as in South Devon. For a time their mode of transport was an old Austin 7, converted to form a van that could transport the brushes.

Mr Ryan Metters recalls that the disposal of the soot was often a problem. At one time there was a rubbish dump that served the Pentewan and Mevagissey areas by the football pitch in Valley Road. On one occasion many years ago he had difficulty carrying the soot, so hit upon the idea of dropping it in the White River at Pentewan. Unexpectedly, it failed to mix with the water and floated away on the surface like strange black ice floes! Fortunately, since then the soot has been taken by a local farmer.

The Boat Builder

There have been a number of boat builders in the area, the following being the most productive: the Luke family at Charlestown from the 1790s to 1874, the Stephens at Fowey (1874–78), while the Moss and Tregaskes families operated from Par from the late 1800s until the 1950s. Meanwhile, Mevagissey had a string of boat builders, the first recorded being Thomas Shepheard in 1786 (who also employed shipwrights at Charlestown), but the tradition continues up to the

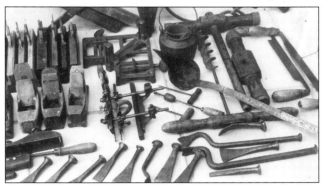

Tools of the boat builders' trade, including caulking irons in the foreground, a variety of planes and an assortment of other hand tools. (Mr W. A. Frazier)

present day with John Moor and his son, Peter.

Mr Arthur Frazier recalls how boats were constructed in the family boatyard of W. Frazier & Son of Mevagissey. The last boat to be constructed there was in 1966; traditional methods and materials were used.

Upstairs in the main shed used for boat building was a drawing loft. Here moulds were 'laid off' (drawn) on the floor onto a board. The plan would then be drawn full size on the board to produce a frame. The keel and stern-posts would be laid out, then supported on blocks so that the water-line was absolutely level. On a 'steam frame carvel hull' (a type of boat hull, formed with the aid of steam) ribbons (battens) would then be attached around the moulds, forming the shape of the hull. A steam boiler would be used to bend Canadian rock elm under pressure to form it to shape, before it was pinned to the mould with copper nails. Then planking could commence, starting with the top strakes (planks) to form the shear (shape of hull). Progressively, the ribbons would then be removed as the planks were added down as far as the bilges (bottom section of the hull). Next the 'garboard' plank was attached to the keel, and planking would continue upwards from that until they reached the bilge. The last plank, the shutter, would finally be spiled in (i.e. fitted) to close the gap. It would take many hours for the copper nails to be firmly riveted using copper washers and a dolly. The hull would be fitted out according to the type of vessel being built.

Mr Frazier recalls that it was labour-intensive work, with six or seven men constructing each craft. Various tasks would be allotted to different craftsmen, depending on their complexity. The journeymen would plane the planks to the correct sizes. Apprentices would gain experience planking. Boys would be given the menial tasks such as fetching and carrying, or powering the hand-driven lathe. It is little wonder that the majority of boats today are made of fibre-glass, as the process is far quicker and involves less specialisation.

References
1 Pigot's 1830 *Directory of Devon and Cornwall*, p.161.
2 *Cornish Guardian*, 19 June 1903, p.9.
3 Pigot's 1830 *Directory of Devon and Cornwall*, p.161.
4 D.B. Barton, *A Historical Survey of the Mines and Mineral Railways of East Cornwall and West Devon*, p.9.
5 F.W.L. Stockdale, *Excursions in the County of Cornwall*, p.49.
6 D.B. Barton, *op. cit.*, p.21.
7 Slater's *Directory of Cornwall 1852–53*, p.50.
8 *Ibid*.
9 D.B. Barton, *op. cit.*, p.17.
10 *Ibid*.
11 A.K. Hamilton Jenkin, *Mines and Miners of Cornwall – VIII. Truro to the Clay District*, p.40.
12 A.K. Hamilton Jenkin, *op. cit.*, p.46

Chapter 8

Local Events

In an age before television and radio, and when people had fewer holidays and less money to spend, many looked forward to the various feast days that took place in and around St Austell. Life in Cornwall was in many ways very different in the early years of the twentieth century. People were content with home-spun amusement, and with most people attending church, and their children attending Sunday school, these institutions often provided their entertainment as well as their enlightenment.

St Austell Feast Week

St Austell Feast Week was the week following Trinity Sunday – the Parish Church being the Holy Trinity Church. On the Monday was Charlestown Regatta (see below). On the Tuesday was Mount Charles Feast when all the Sunday school children were treated to a 'tay-drink' or tea treat. On Wednesday was the Town Feast, with parades, as well as sports events held at Rocky Park, and a tea provided for the children from the various Sunday schools. On Thursday was Trethurgy Feast, while on Friday, which was market-day, things returned to normal.

Mevagissey Feast Week

The week after St Austell Feast was Mevagissey Feast marking St Peter's-tide. This lasted a whole week, as it still does in 2005.

Charlestown Regatta

The format of Charlestown Regatta remains very much unchanged, although Regatta Week took place

in August in 2005. The event of 1929 included the following: swimming, diving for plates, the greasy pole, and sailing races, while Mount Charles Band provided the background music.

Then came what everyone was looking forward to, the water polo semi-final between Looe and St Austell. The teams were: St Austell – Isaacs, Bennetts, Williams, Hendy, Bawden, Wilkinson, Roberts.[1]

St Austell, by the way, won 2-0.

Pentewan Gala Day

Pentewan Gala Day had a similar programme of events, including greasy-pole competitions and water sports. The event died out in the 1950s, but was revived in August 2003, with the addition of modern attractions such as music by local bands, a barbecue and a grand finale of fireworks.

Bethel Chapel Anniversary

Bethel Chapel celebrated its anniversary on Whit Sunday, and on the Monday the feast and sports event took place in the recreation-ground opposite. In 1903 it was recorded in the *Cornish Guardian* that:

Bethel Bible Christian Sunday School festival was concluded on Feast Tuesday. Teachers and scholars met in the Schoolroom at 1.30p.m., formed in procession half an hour later, and (led by the St Austell Volunteer Band) walked to Cuddra, the residence of Mr R.H. Williams. Returning to Holmbush, they met the Charlestown Wesleyan Sunday School and proceeded with them to Mount Charles, continuing through

Greensplatt Sunday school anniversary, pre-1929. (A new building was constructed in that year.) (Mr L. Lean)

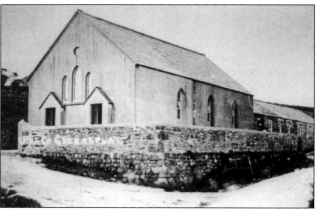

Greensplatt chapel and Sunday school, pre-1929.

(Mr L. Lean)

A tea treat, just prior to or after the First World War. The postcard was produced by Chapman, Mount Charles. (MRS B. WEBBER)

Mount Charles Fife and Drum Band, 'The Band of Hope' of Bridge Chapel, c.1914. The picture is from the 'Vanguard Series' of Chapman, Mount Charles. (MRS B. WEBBER)

Molinnis (Bugle) Fife and Drum Band. Bill Rundle, wearing a top hat, conducts. (MRS J. WILCOCKS)

Victoria-road and back to Bethel by way of Union Road [Clifden Road] and Sandy Bottom.

Anything but ideal conditions prevailed during the latter part of the journey. A terrific thunderstorm burst over the district about 3.30p.m. Vivid flashes of lightning and alarming peals of thunder followed in quick succession, while torrents of hail and rain drove teachers and scholars to every available form of shelter.

Under the genial influence of an excellent tea... there was a general disposition to take a cheerful view of things.[2]

Mount Charles Feast

During Mount Charles Feast the children from Mount Charles Chapel, Bridge Chapel and Primitive Chapel paraded behind the band from Clifden Road to John Lovering's house and beautiful gardens at Polkyth. Here they were entertained by the band. In 2005 this is the site of Polkyth Recreation Centre. A few isolated pines and a magnificent rhododendron, trapped between the swimming-pool and the former YMCA building, remain as testimony to this garden. It was once planted with many fine rhododendrons and included tennis-courts.

Then the children walked to Inch's Field at Cromwell Road to partake of large saffron buns and a cup of tea. They also participated in various races before crossing the road to the fair.

Rescorla Feast Week

Likewise, Rescorla, today a backwater to the north of Penwithick, was significant enough to host its own feast week. This commenced on the last Sunday in June with the annual Sunday school anniversary. The next day the local brass band paraded round the village, followed by children waving flags. The youngsters would then be provided with a 'tea treat' consisting of a large saffron bun and a cup of tea. After a short service in the chapel everyone would congregate in the adjoining Chapel Field where the more athletic would join in the 'Snail Creep', a slow processional dance, which was accompanied by the Molinnis Fife and Drum Band from the nearby hamlet.

Summer Excursions

Chapels often organised annual summer excursions for their congregations. These events were looked forward to with great anticipation, as for many they broke up the monotonous and hard routine of their lives, and gave them an opportunity to venture away from their own neighbourhoods, if only for a day.

The Band of Hope

Members of the Band of Hope had to sign the following pledge:

I Promise by Divine Assistance to abstain from all intoxicating liquors as beverages, and to discountenance all the causes and practices of intemperance.
Signed:
Witness:
Date:

The Greensplatt Band of Hope Pledge Book for 1903–1921 contains lists of wonderful period

Smartly dressed ladies attending Whitemoor chapel women's anniversary, c.May 1939. (MRS D. BILLING)

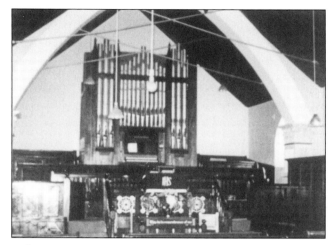

Whitemoor chapel. The organ is to be removed in the near future. (MRS D. BILLING)

Christian names as well as familiar local surnames; the book is beautifully handwritten. Next to several entries has been added in pencil 'Broke', to signify that they had been unable to keep their pledges.

St Austell Flora Day

St Austell Flora Day followed a similar format to Helston's more famous event, which still flourishes at the time of writing. In 1930, when the event was in its third year, the *Cornish Guardian* reported the following:

The route followed was Poltair Recreation Ground, King's Avenue, East Hill, Beech Road, Old House, Church Street, Fore Street, Truro Road, Recreation Ground (Truro Road). Halts were called on the way and deviations were made from the thoroughfares by dancers

through Dr Moore's grounds in Alexandra Road, Old House Gardens, East Hill, and the shops of Mr E.J. Hall, Mr J. Kirk, Star Tea Co., Woolworth's, Mr Sydney Grose, and Messrs S. Hawke and Son.[3]

Unlike Helston, which held a number of different dances at various times throughout the day, such as the children's dance, St Austell held just the one. For this the girls wore white dresses, with sprays of forget-me-nots placed in buttonholes or in their hair bands. The grand finale of the event was described in the *Cornish Guardian* as follows:

At the Truro Road Recreation Ground the grand finale was enacted, the band playing in the centre of the flora dancers encircling them. The daintily dressed girls, the smiling faces of dancers, the delighted onlookers occupying the various points of vantage, with the sun shedding its welcome rays upon the scene against the foliaged background of Trevarrick, presented a picture of great beauty that will linger as a very pleasant memory of a beautiful spectacle.[4]

Sadly, unlike its counterpart in Helston, the St Austell Flora Day was not to survive.

St Austell Hospital Fête

Another annual event was St Austell Hospital Fête, which reached its apogee during the 1920s and 1930s. A week of events took place during August, concluding with a fête at Trevarrick Park, on Hospital Saturday (a fund-raising event). Here ten or more local brass bands would congregate, having marched there from different directions. Then they would accompany the carnival procession as far as Mount

Preparing for the Flora Dance, May 1936. Some of the children are seen here at Mount Charles School with their teacher, Miss Williams. They are holding hands as they danced in fours.

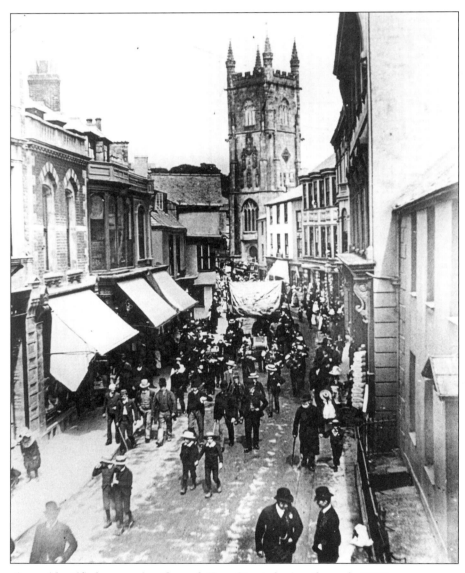

An unidentified procession through Fore Street during the early 1900s.

(Mr M. Stone)

An almost deserted Fore Street, 1930s. The hoarding across the street in front of the church appears to say 'Hospital Fete'.

Greensplatt Band. Sadly the date of the photograph is unknown. (Mr L. Lean)

Greensplatt Band at Stenalees, 1923. (Mr L. Lean)

Charles and back to Trevarrick where a concert would be held. In the evening the event would culminate in a fireworks display. Today St Austell Community Hospital League of Friends raises funds for the hospital, the highlight of the year being the fête in June, held in the grounds at Penrice.

Local Brass Bands

The popularity of local brass bands was probably due to the Band of Hope fife and drum bands. This is a tradition that has continued up to the present day, the county still supporting over 40 brass bands at the time of writing. In 1929 the famous cornet player, Arthur Laycock, performed as a soloist at a concert with St Austell Band. Tragically, he collapsed shortly afterwards and died in hospital the next day. Like many other pastimes, the activities of St Austell Band were disrupted by the Second World War and, as so many players had been called up, the St Austell Area Scratch Band was formed. This included such players as Frank Arthur, Frank Brewer, Maurice Burt, Walter Bailey and Cecil Brewer when they were able to participate. Cecil Brewer later became musical director of the band, replacing C.H. Baker, who had been appointed in 1938, and held the position until 1961 when he moved to Mount Charles Band. (He was musical director there until 1966.)

At one time there would have been far more local bands: villages such as Greensplatt, Foxhole, Stenalees and Mevagissey each had their own. Like Bugle, Stenalees used to host an open-air band contest, but this died out along with the band in the early 1960s. An attempt to revive the Stenalees band during the 1980s was unsuccessful. As with the Band of Hope, they had their own code of rules set out in a booklet in which it was specified that smoking and bad language would be frowned upon. As well as participating in competitions and concerts, the bands led processions and played at tea treats, local fêtes and sports days. St Austell Band Room in East Hill was opened in 1911.

May Day/Labour Day

Each year May Day or Labour Day was also celebrated in St Austell. In 1926, for example:

... the local Labour Party arranged an extensive programme of sports including a football tournament, which took place at the St Austell football field. Unfortunately the wild and wet weather made greatly against the sports but, considering the conditions, quite a large number attended.[5]

Alexandra Rose Day

Another local event which no longer exists is Alexandra Rose Day. Once celebrated on 24 June, on this day pink artificial roses were sold and the proceeds went to the nurses. In 1936, for example, a total of £70 was raised. The event was named after the nurses' patron, Princess Alexandra.

St Austell's Day

St Austell's Day was once celebrated on a Saturday in August and often commenced in the Market House with the crowning of the carnival queen. This event has also been consigned to history.

Travelling Shows and Fairs

The Fair Park was an integral part of the town, situated at the junction of Truro Road and Gover Road, opposite Richards & Dyer's bakery and next to Hill & Phillips's Motor Works. A series of travelling shows came to the park, the principal one after the First World War and throughout the 1920s being the Bristol-based Hancock's, then the largest amusement caterers in the West Country; they even had a traction engine built to combat the Cornish hills. After their demise in 1926, they were followed by Anderton & Rowlands and Whiteleggs from Plymouth.

The occasional circus also appeared from time to time, although when the large Bertram Mills circus came in 1938 they were accommodated at Rocky Park, home to the speedway racing and Captain Percy Phillips' landing field. When the Bertram Mills circus came again in 1957 they went to the rugby ground on the bypass, which is now the location of Asda supermarket. The site of the Fair Park has since become an industrial complex.

St Austell Tennis Week

The area has found enthusiastic support for a wide range of sporting activities over the years, whether one was a participant, or a spectator. An example of this is St Austell Tennis Week which was inaugurated in 1927.

Boxing

Boxing was staged at a number of local venues. For example, in 1929 the following bout took place:

A large number of St Austell enthusiasts gathered at Mr Sam Mc Keown's boxing booth at the Fair Park, St Austell, on Saturday night, when Frank Radcliffe, the Cornish champion, was matched in a ten two-minute round contest with Tom O'Neill, described as 'The Plymouth Idol'.[6]

O'Neill's better hitting 'gained him the verdict on a small margin of points'.[7]

Bertram Mills circus had already performed to large audiences in Newquay for three days before travelling 'in its four special trains and road transport convoys to St Austell' where it would stay for another three days (advertised in the Cornish Guardian, 15 August 1957, p.8).

The circus comes to town in 1938. A cart pulled by oxen makes its way down Bypass Road.

(MR W. PAPPIN)

Circus elephants processing
down Bypass Road, 1938.

(MR W. PAPPIN)

St Austell AFC

St Austell and many of the surrounding villages have their own football teams. St Austell AFC, the 'Lilywhites', used to be very well supported, and large crowds would gather at the football field at Poltair until well into the 1950s to support their local sides. Occasional visits by such stars as Sir Stanley Matthews, or John and Mel Charles, as well as successes in League Championships, helped swell the numbers.

St Austell AFC, 1937–38, Left to right, back row: H. Bishop, Fred Lobb, Bill Lobb, Harry Monk, Tom Atkinson (goalkeeper), Bill Tout, Ted Griffiths, Jack Webber (secretary); front row: ? Avery, ? French, Lloyd Sweet, Phil Smith, Les Pollard. (MRS B. WEBBER)

The football team, seen here leaving the Bull Ring in 1920, to play a final at Bodmin. The Red Bank is in the background. (MR W. PAPPIN)

Football legend John Charles (front row, fourth from left) *and his brother Mel played in an exhibition match at St Austell in 1957. Their opponents were a team made up of some Plymouth Argyle players as well some county players and local club footballers. A week later John Charles was transferred to Juventus in Italy for £65,000 – although playing for St Austell probably had little to do with it!*

(Mr R. Dutch)

Footballer John Charles was clearly very popular with the youngsters when he played for St Austell in 1954. He is seen here signing autographs afterwards. (Mr R. Dutch)

St Austell Rifle and Pistol Club

Behind the football stadium, a purpose-built shooting range and hall was created for St Austell Rifle and Pistol Club in 1964, which has also proved to be a valuable venue for other activities as well.

Car and Motorcycle Racing

In 1949 a new speedway track opened at Par Moor, with the local Gulls team being very popular. Races against visiting international teams were attended by crowds running into the thousands. Later, stock car and banger events took over, before the site was redeveloped for retail use in the 1980s.

St Austell & District Scooter Club

In July 1957 St Austell & District Scooter Club was founded, with the club headquarters in a disused barn at Cooperage Farm, Trewoon.[8] Sadly, the popularity of this form of transport would wane, as would the club it was founded upon.

St Austell and District Rifle and Pistol Club dinner, held at Duporth Farm Hotel, 1958/59.

(MID CORNWALL PHOTOGRAPHIC SERVICES C/O MR T. A DYER)

A sea of sails as the Dart 18 sailing competition is held at Pentewan Sands on 1 June 1994.

The area that was once known as 'The Winnick' at Pentewan was laid out with marquees to provide hospitality for the sailing event, clearly sponsored by Citroën.

1st St Austell Cub Scout Group, c.1935. The photograph includes: *Miss Marriot and Henry Rickard (assistant cub leader).*

St Austell Amateur Operatic Society's performance of The Desert Song *at the Capitol Theatre, on 15 March 1947, the first show to be put on after the Second World War. Mr D.J. Kellow plays Red Shadow.*

(MRS I. HANCOCK)

The Sound of Music was showing at the Capitol on 28 September 1967 (advertised in the Cornish Guardian *of that day).*

St Austell Amateur Operatic Society

St Austell Amateur Operatic Society has been a successful organisation, putting on annual productions since its foundation in 1916, apart from when the Second World War intervened. Performances have taken place at the Capitol Theatre, St Austell Arts Centre at Truro Road, Cornwall Coliseum at Carlyon Bay and now the newly built theatre, The Keay.

Carol Singing

Aylmer Square was an ideal venue for carol singing at Christmas time. When the square was created a covered pipe was sunk into the ground in which the Christmas tree could be positioned each year. On one occasion when the lights were being set up on the tree a smartly dressed official in a sharp suit turned up and demanded to know why the tree had been stuck into a drain. He ordered the electricians to stop work immediately and remain just where they were. They knew about the pipe, and with wry smiles on their faces sat down on the staging while the official stormed off towards Somerset House. He returned shortly afterwards with two other suited gentlemen, who being somewhat wiser, surveyed the scene and were able to reassure everyone that all was well!

Royal Visits

Over the years St Austell has hosted a number of royal visits. These include a visit by George V and Queen Mary to South Goonbarrow clay works (as well as Bodmin) in April 1935. On 29 October 1947

King George VI and Queen Elizabeth visited mid-Cornwall. During the tour they went to Carnsmerry, Bugle, to inspect 30 new 'Cornish Unit' houses. Mr and Mrs Maurice Crowle had the honour of showing the royal couple around their new home.

The Duke of Edinburgh visited the china clay district in October 1952 and opened the new recreation-ground at Whitemoor.

A reporter for the *Cornish Guardian* grew very excited when the royal yacht *Britannia* anchored in St Austell Bay for the night on the return journey from a royal tour of the Commonwealth in 1954:

A new page was added to the history of the St Austell area. The St Austell Bay was chosen as the haven for Britannia *and her proud escort of warships on Thursday night.[9]*

On 6 May 1961, the Duke of Edinburgh arrived by helicopter to visit St Austell Grammar School and the clay works. Five years later Queen Elizabeth II arrived by train at St Austell Station to be greeted by officials and large crowds of locals waving flags.

The Queen's silver jubilee on 7 June 1977 was celebrated with many local events and street parties. One of the more long-standing benefits to result from the jubilee was the creation of a shoppers' car park and small garden at Tregonissey Lane End on what had previously been unkempt wasteland, and paid for by local fund-raising.

It is likely that Prince Charles made at least one unofficial visit to the late Dr A.L. Rowse at his home at Trenarren not long before his death in 1997.

References
[1] *Cornish Guardian*, 1 August 1929, p.12.
[2] *Cornish Guardian*, 19 June 1903, p.9.
[3] *Cornish Guardian*, 3 July 1930, p.14.
[4] *Ibid*.
[5] *Cornish Guardian*, 7 May 1926, p.4.
[6] *Cornish Guardian*, 14 March 1929, p.4.
[7] *Ibid*.
[8] *Cornish Guardian*, 19 September 1957, p.9.
[9] *Cornish Guardian*, 20 May 1954, p.8.

Four Santas! Surely not? Left to right: *Robert Isaacs, Jim Brewer, ?, Owen Richards.* (MR O. RICHARDS)

Holy Trinity Church and Christmas lights during the early 1990s, seen from Market Street. (MR T.J. WHETTER)

Royal visitors in Fore Street, c.1910.

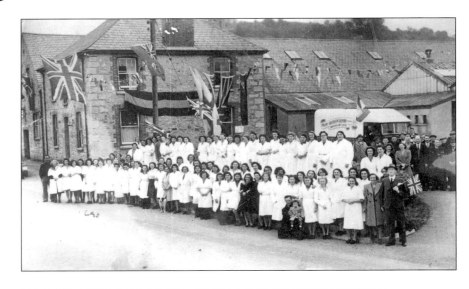

The staff of Moon's Laundry, St Blazey, awaiting a royal visit, 1947. (MR M. STONE)

The floral arch at the bottom of High Cross Street, between The Red Bank and the Rural District Council offices, to welcome King George VI and Queen Elizabeth, October 1947.

(MR D. STONE)

The royal visit of George VI and Queen Elizabeth. They are seen here leaving a new Cornish Unit at Bugle in October 1947. The King's car is on the right.

(MR M. STONE)

Another view of the royal visit in October 1947. The royal car is nearest the building.
(MR M. STONE)

The arrival of the royal party, October 1947. The crowds cheered and waved their handkerchiefs.
(MR M. STONE)

Mr W.G. Scone visits Carclaze chapel in June 1953, to attend a ceremony to mark the coronation of Elizabeth II. The photograph was taken by local photographer, Roy Dutch.

(Mr R. Dutch)

HRH The Duke of Edinburgh opened the new recreation-ground at Whitemoor on 30 October 1952. Mr Meade-King, a director of English China Clay Ltd, is on the right. The recreation-ground included a children's area with swings, a see-saw and sand pit, as well as an adult area.

(Mrs D. Billing)

HRH The Duke of Edinburgh seen arriving at the entrance to the playing-fields in 1952. The clay workings make a striking background, while the Austin car and the women in hats date the picture.

(Mrs D. Billing)

Queen Elizabeth II arrives at St Austell Station for a royal visit on 14 July 1966. Many locals came to greet her, including schoolchildren who had time off to wave their flags in welcome. The day return fares offered by British Railways at the time were: Camborne, 9s.; Truro, 5s.; Plymouth, 13s.6d. Her Majesty was to tour the Clay Country, visit RAF St Mawgan, as well as open the new County Hall in Truro. (MR R. DUTCH)

Queen Elizabeth II signing a visitors' book during her tour of the area in 1966. (MR R. DUTCH)

Chapter 9
Responding to External Events

St Austell is situated in the far south-west of the country, on the south coast of a peninsula reaching out into the sea and geographically remote from large centres of population. However, this hasn't guaranteed it immunity from involvement in national and international events, often events that offered no advantage to the town or its population.

Defending the Town

St Austell's location on the South Coast meant that it was often in danger of attack from the Continent. During the fourteenth and fifteenth-centuries Fowey was attacked and burnt by the French, leading to Place House assuming its present form with fortifications. During the Tudor period St Catherine's Castle was constructed to protect the mouth of the river. When Charles Rashleigh constructed the harbour at Charlestown at the end of the eighteenth century, he arranged for it to be defended against Napoleonic France by Crinnis Cliff Battery (sometimes called Charlestown Gun Battery) which looked down on the entrance. The battery was equipped with four 18-pound cannons until 1860, when they were upgraded to 24-pounders; later these were replaced with 32-pounders with a range of two miles. The estate workers were formed into a company of artillery volunteers, and held regular gun-drill until 1896.

(The term 'volunteer' was a misnomer: it secured the landlord a workforce, making them exempt from conscription.)

During the twentieth century the whole coastline was dotted with pillboxes, as well as the occasional gun emplacement and watchtower, to repel a German invasion.

Disease

Pestilence and disease was often an unwelcome visitor to the area. For example, when a cholera epidemic struck Mevagissey in 1849, possibly brought there by a visiting sailor, many residents fled to Polkirt and slept in tents until the pestilence had passed. Nonetheless, some 115 people died in just five weeks. The burial-ground for victims in the cemetery could not be disturbed for a century because of the risk of contamination.

In June 1904 the *Cornish Guardian* reported that:

Dr Mason, medical officer of health, stated that during the month no infectious or contagious diseases had been notified to him. This is a most gratifying announcement, and speaks volumes for the vigilance of the medical officer and the sanitary inspector (Mr T. Darlington) and also the Council, whose capacity for expediting business is well known.

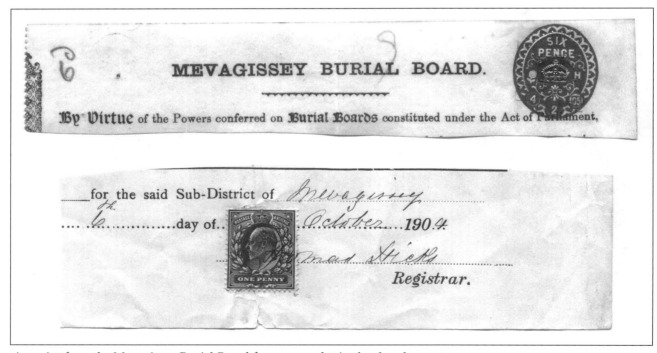

A receipt from the Mevagissey Burial Board for a grave plot in the church cemetery.

The Council is to be heartily congratulated upon the fact that in such a large and populous district not a single infections [sic] case has occurred.[1]

In October 1918 there was a rabies scare in Plymouth, and there were fears that it might spread in to Cornwall.[2]

The First World War

As a result of a series of seemingly remote events in Europe, Britain declared war on Germany on 4 August 1914. An early casualty of the First World War was Richard Charles Graves Sawle, a Lieutenant of the Coldstream Regiment of Footguards, who was killed at Ypres in Belgium on 2 November 1914. As a memorial to his only son, in 1921 Rear Admiral Sir Charles Graves Sawle of Penrice gave Menacuddle Baptistry and the surrounding land to the parish.

In December 1914 some 370 soldiers were billeted in the town, although they were not foisted on the private residents:

Nearly all the public buildings in the town have been requisitioned for the purpose. These include the Wesleyan School premises, the Public Rooms, including the Drill Hall there, the Lecture Hall [Trevarthian Road], the Territorial Drill Hall, Mr Venning's store at East Hill, the Baptist Schoolroom, the Working Men's Club Room of South Street, and other places.[3]

The soldiers were offered use of the football field for drill practice. During this stage of the conflict newspapers were full of jingoistic reports from the Front, anti-German rhetoric and recruitment campaigns, as well as lists of soldiers, many members of the DCLI (Duke of Cornwall's Light Infantry), who had been killed or were missing in action.

On 7 May 1915 the passenger liner *Lusitania* was torpedoed by a U-boat off the coast of southern Ireland. She sank 18 minutes later with the loss of 1,198 lives. Mr F.J. Milford was the only St Austell man on board, and he managed to escape in a lifeboat, 'none the worse for his thrilling adventure, but bereft of all belongings except his watch, and a single suit of clothes'.[4]

In the same edition of the *Cornish Guardian* a photograph appeared of a group of 'Tregonissey boys' in India.[5] No doubt it provided much needed reassurance that they were alive and well, and did local recruitment no harm either.

Captain the Hon. Thomas C.R. Agar-Robartes

In October 1915 came the tragic news that Captain the Hon. Thomas C.R. Agar-Robartes, MP for St Austell, had been killed on the Western Front. He was just 35 years old. The fourth MP to be killed up

until that time, he was succeeded as MP for mid-Cornwall by Sir Francis Layland-Barrett.

The eldest son of Viscount Cliften of Lanhydrock, Agar-Robartes had been educated at Eton and Christ Church, Oxford. He had contemplated entering the Army in 1903 when he left university, but settled instead on a political career. A respected MP, at the outbreak of war he had been keen to get to the Front, so transferred from the Devon Yeomanry to the Buckinghamshires. Then he secured a commission in the Coldstream Guards as a lieutenant, being later gazetted a captain.

Agar-Robartes had already been wounded in May 1915, but by 30 September he was at the village of Loos. In the fourth battle there, which was 'a severe hand-to-hand fight, he was leading his men when he was shot at close quarters, through the left lung by an expanding bullet'.[6] He died the following morning and, after a Church of England service, was buried near the battlefield. There is a fine memorial in his honour in Truro Cathedral which states that for rescuing a wounded comrade under heavy fire he was recommended for the Victoria Cross. He is commemorated in St Austell by a plaque on the corner of Park Road and Truro Road, as well as in the street names, Agar Road and Robartes Place.

A short time before Agar-Robartes left for France, Liberal agent, Mr H. Syd Hancock[7] had met him at Lanhydrock and expressed the hope that he would come back safe. Sadly and prophetically Agar-Robartes had replied, 'No; if you go over there, and see what I have seen you would never dream of coming back again'.[8]

In a full-page obituary the *Cornish Guardian* jingoistically announced, 'The death was grand, the cause was just'.[9] No doubt the reporter did not want to put off any potential heroes.

Recruitment and Training

At that time recruiting was continuing apace, with young men urged to sign up by the famous pointing finger of Lord Kitchener, a letter in local newspapers from King George V, as well as Lord Derby's recruiting scheme which marked young men out as 'starred' if they had a valid reason for not signing up, or 'unstarred' if they had not yet done so. It must have been very difficult for anyone with doubts about the validity of the cause to avoid the call up, and for those who tried to be misrepresented there were severe penalties. Those who had not already seen it as their duty to enlist were forced to face their consciences:

The town and Mount Charles district have been well done and there are very few single men now left to be recruited. In the clay district there are still many single men who could be spared, but who have shown no disposition to answer the country's call.[10]

GUARDIAN, FRIDAY, OCTOBER 29, 1915.

BUCKINGHAM PALACE.

TO MY PEOPLE.

At this grave moment in the struggle between my people and a highly organised enemy who has transgressed the Laws of Nations and changed the ordinance that binds civilized Europe together, I appeal to you.

I rejoice in my Empire's effort, and I feel pride in the voluntary response from my Subjects all over the world who have sacrificed home fortune, and life itself, in order that another may not inherit the free Empire which their ancestors and mine have built.

I ask you to make good these sacrifices.

The end is not in sight. More men and yet more are wanted to keep my Armies in the Field, and through them to secure Victory and enduring peace.

In ancient days the darkest moment has ever produced in men of our race the sternest resolve.

I ask you, men of all classes, to come forward voluntarily and take your share in the fight.

In freely responding to my appeal, you will be giving your support to our brothers, who, for long months, have nobly upheld Britain's past traditions, and the glory of her Arms.

George R.I.

A recruitment message from King George V (from the Cornish Guardian, *29 October 1915, p.7).*

A group of First World War soldiers in 1918. The photograph includes: Lance Corporal E.R. (Roy) Hugo (back row, sixth from left). In 1917 he had fought in the Battle of Cambrai, the first major engagement involving tanks. He returned to St Austell injured, keeping the large piece of shrapnel that had been removed as a souvenir. He later ran a general food shop and butcher's in Truro Road.

(Mr P. Clemo)

Farmers as well as clay workers were marked out as those shirking their responsibilities, and the article went into details about what would happen to them under Lord Derby's scheme if there was conscription later on. However, the campaign of intimidation continued to bear fruit, and a week later it was reported that: 'It is calculated that something approaching 1,000 men passed through the St Austell recruiting office in the last two days of the campaign'.[11]

Meanwhile at home, training continued. It was reported in January 1918 that: 'The men of the 13th and 14th Platoons of D Co., St Austell, took part in a service rifle competition on Trenarren Range'.[12]

There was also a rifle range on Crinnis Beach long before the First World War, the 1907 Ordnance Survey map clearly showing the target located against the cliffs behind the site of the Coliseum.

Local Methodists in the Forces

By October 1918, a month before the Armistice was signed, in an article about St Austell United Methodists it was reported that '806 from the circuit had joined his Majesty's Forces, 65 having made the supreme sacrifice, 86 wounded, four missing, and five prisoners in Germany'.[13]

The Armistice

The Armistice was greeted with great jubilation. Dr A.L. Rowse recalled, 'I remember the momentary

A card sent to Roy Hugo by his 'Affectionate Brother', Gordon, from Shoeburyness on 25 July 1917. He is photographed in his uniform before an unconvincing canvas backdrop, and perhaps wondered if he would see his family again.

(Mr P. Clemo)

return to the old ways, for we celebrated the Armistice with a Flora Dance through the town'. By then hardly anyone could remember the correct steps, so that, 'we just crowded the narrow, tortuous Fore Street of St Austell town, treading on each other's heels in a snake-walk'.[14] There was a public outpouring of euphoria at the end of the terrible conflict:

Never was there such a crush as in our town on the night of November 11th, 1918; the old instinctive impulse brought in hundreds, thousands from all the villages round, from the populous china clay district, and as the night wore on the little twisting street was impassable, jammed with happy, released humanity.[15]

The cessation of hostilities was in many ways the end of an era. Many of the old customs, along with the social order and the public's political naivety also died on the battlefields of Flanders.

The General Strike

In May 1926 the country faced a fresh crisis, the General Strike. The effect on St Austell was mixed, although even those who did not follow their union's call to down tools faced the anxiety of shortages. The *Cornish Guardian* tried to allay fears by announcing:

Arrangements for maintaining essential supplies and services in the St Austell area are well in hand. For the moment it is stated that supplies available are sufficient to meet normal requirements.[16]

The majority of china clay workers did come out on strike. Many of the works still had stocks of clay and were well supplied with coal to continue operating the dries. However, there was another problem:

The transport of china clay by rail was at a standstill and the loading of vessels with china clay at Fowey was suspended at six o'clock in the morning after the finish of the night shift.[17]

For the populace of the town, the GWR was able to maintain a bus service between St Austell and Bodmin and for many life carried on as normal. The General Strike was not as universal as might be supposed. There were also other outlets for china clay:

The dockers at Charlestown who remained at work all last week state that they received no official notification

Fore Street and Holy Trinity Church, 1960.

Approaching Carlyon Bay Hotel along the coastal footpath from Charlestown, c.1930. (MR W. PAPPIN)

of the strike from their union and therefore did not withdraw their labour.[18]

Later an attempt was made to persuade them to down tools, but their answer was that given 'a choice between striking or severing their connections with the union, they prefer the latter'.[19] The port continued to be busy, and was in fact handling more coastal vessels as a consequence of the embargo at other home ports. Nor was the stoppage on the railways having any effect:

All the clay being shipped at Charlestown is coming by road from works adjacent to St Austell – the method of transport always adopted in consequence of neither the works nor the port being on the railway.[20]

The situation at Par was somewhat different. There was a brief stoppage, but Colonel Edward Treffry, the proprietor of the port, called a meeting and said that if they didn't resume work, 'their places would be permanently filled by other men and their services would be no longer required'.[21]

In fact, on the Friday when the events of the previous week were being publicised, it was also announced that the General Strike had been terminated on the previous Wednesday afternoon. The columnist also proudly reported:

It is rather remarkable that the good news was known in Cornwall at least ten minutes before the general public in London were aware of what had happened – another example of the wonderful advantages of wireless.[22]

The Second World War

The Second World War affected young and old alike. In the early days there was a large influx of evacuees escaping the bombing in the industrial cities. Billets were found in spare rooms of people's houses, and home-owners had little choice but to take them in, regardless of their own needs or prejudices. Sutton Boys' School from Plymouth was evacuated to Tremena House which was at Menacuddle. Hotels were also commandeered: King's School from Canterbury stayed at the Cliff Head and Carlyon Bay Hotel.

Local children had to become accustomed to the presence of 'strangers', with unusual accents, manners and customs, sharing their schools. An interesting insight into the effect of the war can be learnt from reading the logbook of West Hill School. Events occurring in 1938, before the war began, are recorded as follows:

April 25th
There are a few cases of Mumps, especially among the girls from the Scattered Homes [homes for displaced children].

May 24th
Empire Day was observed from 11a.m. to 12 noon today, when the assembled school joined in appropriate songs & recitations & listened to an Empire Address from Revd F.A. Bond, curate of the Parish Church.

June 14th
Mount Charles Feast: holiday this afternoon.[23]

Soon events were to unfold that would signal the end of the British Empire and colonialism. Some of the difficulties encountered by those running the school at the time are also revealed:

July 1939
When the St Mewan school was decapitated in January of this year 29 girls were transferred here; the number on the roll has not however altered substantially since the last report.

The school is now organised in six classes, three of which form an 'A' stream & three a 'B' stream. Two of the 'B' classes are at present housed in recently acquired temporary accommodation in the adjoining Baptist Church building; the cramped conditions to which attention was drawn in the last report have thus to some extent been alleviated. It is now possible for each class to have a separate room & to keep the sizes of the 'B' groups within suitable limits...[24]

By the beginning of 1940, the effects of the war were being felt during a period known as the 'phony war' when nothing seemed to happen. Ordinary school routine was beginning to suffer:

January 31st
The gas masks of all scholars overhauled by an A.R.P. warden.

May 15th
About 1.15p.m. one of the evacuee boys was throwing stones & broke the glass above the entrance door to the Baptist Schoolroom. The broken glass fell into the porch: one piece struck Marcia Rowe & slightly cut her forehead.

Whitemoor Home Guard, looking efficient and smart in their uniforms, c.1941. It is interesting to note the predominantly younger element of the company, perhaps because they were in reserved occupations.

(Mrs D. Billing)

Members of the Women's Royal Voluntary Service of Whitemoor in their berets and pinnies, happy in their work preparing a meal in a mobile kitchen. Mrs Damerell is pictured (second from right).

(Mrs D. Billing)

St Austell Youth Rally held at the recreation-ground. Captain Fredenberger of the US Army is carrying out an inspection on 11 May 1944.

(Mrs I. Hancock)

July 5th
Work suspended twice to take cover from air raids during the morning session.

July 10th
Work stopped from 9a.m. to 10a.m. to take cover from air raid.

October 16th
Two A.R.P. wardens have spent the morning in school fixing the Contex [filters] to the scholars' gas masks.

£3-8-0 has been collected by the scholars to help the local 'Spitfire' fund.

November 26th
Work again interrupted by two air-raid warnings, necessitating the scholars & teachers taking refuge in the shelters.[25]

There was another air-raid warning two days later, and lessons were disrupted on several occasions throughout the first three months of 1941 and from February to April 1943. The air raids then continued sporadically until July 1944. Most of the air raids were of the 'tip-and-run' variety, with German pilots dropping surplus bombs on return journeys, or were merely effective in that they caused fear and general disruption.

The first bombs to fall in the area were near The Grove at Charlestown, when on 5 July 1940 three high-explosive bombs fell harmlessly into a field. However, on the night of 13/14 April 1941, and on the following day, Par Harbour was targeted. One house was demolished and cottages at Spit were damaged, along with electrical cables. A house was demolished in an attack at Gover on 9 May 1941, while six bombs fell on Carn Farm, damaging some buildings, and killing three sheep. On 21 November 1941 one enemy plane flew over the town for almost half an hour, possibly looking for the goods' yard or the railway line, and finally dropped two bombs which badly damaged houses in Alexandra Road.

The local Spitfire Fund was successful in raising the £5,000 required and a Spitfire Mk. 1, serial number R7116, was purchased that year and was used by the Photographic Reconnaissance Unit (PRU) operating from St Eval. Sadly it was shot down over the Channel Islands in November 1942, but the pilot survived.[26]

Other events occurred in the war years which affected school life but were of a more pleasant nature. The following examples occurred in 1943:

March 18th
Classes IL & IP this afternoon visited the exhibition at the Public Rooms in connection with the Aid to Russia & Aid to China Week.
[Other classes from the school visited the following day.]

July 6th
Twenty girls, in charge of Miss Pitts, this afternoon visited the 'Mend & Make-Do Exhibition' arranged by the Cornwall Education Committee at the Church Schoolroom.[27]
[The schoolroom was then in South Street, next to the Masonic Hall.]

Other facilities in the area were taken over for war work. The Corn Exchange, built in 1859 and with a fine spiral staircase, was used by the Ministry of Supply. (The building was demolished in December 1960 when the road was widened.) Amphibious craft of the Royal Navy were moored securely at Pentewan Harbour. German POWs were camped at Lanescot. Many of them worked on local farms.

The Royal Indian Service Corps

The 25 Animal Transport Company of the Royal Indian Service Corps came to Duporth Camp in October 1940. Whilst the majority were in their twenties, about 30 of them had served in the First World War and were decorated with 1914–18 Star and General Service and Victory medals. At the beginning of 1941, the 25 Animal Transport Company, as they were then called, moved to Devon, and in October 1941 Mule Company Number 7 arrived. British officers were attached to the units.

Many older residents of the town recall the Indian soldiers and their mules, for they were a curious and rather alien sight in their turbans. Many spoke good English. They used the old Savoy cinema in Truro Road, watered their mules in the stream at Brick Hill (Duporth Road) and participated in fund-raising activities for the war effort, such as parades during 'Salute the Soldier Week' in St Austell.

Tragically, in November 1940, three Indian troops were killed when, during a storm, a large tree was blown down onto one of the chalets in which they were sleeping. They were buried – facing east – at Campdown cemetery. An onlooker recalls that during the funeral procession the mourners wore striped suits and carried poles which they banged together.

Local Defence Volunteers

Mr Frank Authers, who was serving at St Eval in 1940/41, used to come over to St Austell on a Saturday night to attend dances. He recalls an enterprising local baker who would walk along Fore Street carrying a wicker basket on his arm selling hot pasties, the only source of food at that late hour. As a security measure cars had to be disabled during the war, and on one night his friend, 'Ginger' Freethy, could not find the rotor arm of his old car when the time came to return to base. Eventually, after a lot of explaining, the local police helped them out. Then, in what could have been from a scene straight out of *Dad's Army*, they got lost on the return journey, and with the road signs removed, at a checkpoint manned by Local Defence Volunteers (the forerunners of the Home Guard) they were refused directions in case they were spies dressed in RAF uniforms!

The Suez Crisis

In 1956, with Britain in the middle of the Suez Crisis, and with fuel in short supply, there were concerns about its affect on the tourist industry. Gales had already wreaked havoc at camp-sites around St Austell Bay in July. However, there was widespread relief when petrol rationing ended the following spring, although visitors were planning alternative ways of reaching their holiday destination:

Hotels in the St Austell area, such as those at Carlyon Bay, are quite satisfied with the bookings they have received for June...

One of the main reasons why their fears have not been realised is the British Railways car-ferry service from Paddington to St Austell. Hoteliers report that many more people are coming by train this year.[28]

However, hotels that were not so easily served by the railway were to take longer to recover from the fuel crisis:

Mr E.G. Wood, of the Cliff Head Hotel, Carlyon Bay, says his bookings for June are up to normal, which is 'fairly good'. At the beginning of petrol rationing he was worried about the June bookings, but since the petrol position has eased the bookings had improved.

Hotel keepers in Mevagissey are, so far, having a lean season. To them ample petrol for their customers is an essential; without it the season is dead.[29]

The Swinging Sixties

St Austell was to survive the 'Swinging Sixties', with all that the exuberant decade embodied, relatively unscathed. One lasting epitaph has remained on the town's skyline as a legacy of the period's architectural style: the Park House flats. Even from its conception the development was not without its critics though, as an announcement in the *Cornish Guardian* reveals: 'St Austell's controversial proposal to build a 12-storey block of flats at Bridge Road, St Austell, has received Government approval'.[30]

The design was somewhat ameliorated by the fact that the flats were located at the bottom of the hill. Most locals have come to accept the building as a part of the townscape while perhaps feeling grateful that it is the only structure reaching so far into the sky.

References

[1] *Cornish Guardian*, 10 June 1904, p.5.
[2] *Royal Cornwall Gazette*, 30 October 1918, p.7.
[3] *Cornish Guardian*, 18 December 1914, p.8.
[4] *Cornish Guardian*, 14 May 1915, p.7.
[5] *Ibid.*, p.5.
[6] *Cornwall County News*, 13 October 1915, p.7.
[7] Mr H. Sydney Hancock was an important – and busy – local figure himself. Kelly's *Directory of Cornwall* of 1897 lists him as follows: running the firm, Hancock & Sons, auctioneers; clerk of St Austell School Board; assessor and collector of taxes for St Austell parish; Liberal registration agent for St Austell division; secretary to the Liberal Association and to the Cottage Gardening Society and sheriff's officer, Sydney Place.
[8] *Cornish Guardian*, 15 October 1915, p.2.
[9] *Cornish Guardian*, 8 October 1915, p.5.
[10] *Cornish Guardian*, 10 December 1915, p.5.
[11] *Cornish Guardian*, 17 December 1915, p.5.
[12] *Cornwall County News*, 2 January 1918, p.3.
[13] *Royal Cornwall Gazette*, 9 October 1918, p.3
[14] A.L. Rowse, *A Cornish Childhood*, p.7
[15] *Ibid.*
[16] *Cornish Guardian*, 7 May 1926, p.9.
[17] *Ibid.*
[18] *Cornish Guardian*, 14 May 1926, p.8
[19] *Ibid.*
[20] *Ibid.*
[21] *Ibid.*
[22] *Cornish Guardian*, 14 May 1926, p.7.
[23] From the logbook of West Hill School, Cornwall Record Office, Truro, recorded as 'Records of St Austell Evacuee School (Council, mixed)'.
[24] *Ibid.*
[25] *Ibid.*
[26] Peter Hancock, *Cornwall at War*, p.71–72.
[27] Logbook of West Hill School.
[28] *Cornish Guardian*, 16 May 1957, p.5.
[29] *Ibid.*
[30] *Cornish Guardian*, 6 April 1967, p.13.

Chapter 10

Changing Times

New Housing Estates

It can be argued that the largest changes to St Austell occurred during the late-twentieth century, and that the pace of change is still increasing all the time. As large housing estates have been developed on the fringes of the town, the population has risen dramatically. What were once outlying villages, such as Mount Charles, Bethel, Cuddra and Tregonissey, have been absorbed into the urban conurbation.

The area to the south of Tregonissey Road was once open fields and woodland with a stream running through it. Dr A.L. Rowse, in his book *A Cornish Childhood*, describes it affectionately as 'Lost House' or 'Lost Wood'. For him it was a quiet retreat where he could read, or write poetry. (He speculated that the name did not have the obvious meaning but was derived from the Cornish word *Lis*, meaning court or palace.)[1] Towards the end of the book, when writing of the early 1920s, he mentions that council-houses were being built there.

The village itself was changing; across the road the elm-trees, in which I had often heard the winter winds roar while I wrote at night, were coming down to make way for new, unfamiliar houses; the thatched cottages in the garden... had gone.[2]

Trelawney Road was also cut through to link Tregonissey with Slades Road ('Long Lane') during this period: older people referred to it as New Road.

The second half of the twentieth century saw large housing estates sprawling ever further out from the

Hay fields gave way to housing as bungalows were built at Agar Road during the 1960s. This photograph shows the backs of houses in Gwallon Road, with Carlyon Bay and the sea in the distance. (MR R. DUTCH)

Julian & Son (from Harding's Guide Map to the District of St Austell, c.1920s).

town. In 1967 houses on the Wimpey estate at Biscovey were advertised 'For Value & Views', and then priced at £3,125.[3] In 1980 new houses at Parkway were available from £21,650, while at the same time those at Edgcumbe Green were for sale from £28,750. In 2005, even an old clay dry at Carclaze is being turned into 27 luxury apartments, as part of Wainhomes' Lovering Fields development on the site of the old sawmills. Similarly, outlying villages have swelled in order to cope with the demand for new houses.

Restoration of Former Clay Pits

The Aberfan Disaster of 1966 – when a coal tip collapsed after heavy rain, burying a school in South Wales – was not just a wake-up call for the coal industry, but for other extraction industries as well. Since then the 'Cornish Alps' which once formed the backdrop to the town have gradually become less intrusive, as clay tips have been reshaped, greened over, and old pits filled in. Previously, the nine tonnes of waste produced during the acquisition of every tonne of clay was simply heaped up into ever-expanding tips via growing runs of conveyor belts that snaked across the downs. Modern clay companies are paying more attention to the effect of their industry on the landscape.

One of the first restoration projects was the back-filling of the huge Menear Pit, known locally as Buckey Pit, north-east of Phernyssick. This ancient opencast tin mine was restored to grazing land in 1978–80 and there is now no trace of it.

The old sawmills site at Carclaze in August 2003.

Trevarth, Mevagissey, in 1916. The houses were owned by professional and retired folk. The photograph was taken by Mevagissey photographer, Jules Toullec, who had a studio on Polkirt Hill.

In the 1990s Caerloggas Pit, to the north of Penwithick, was filled in by Imerys and the surrounding tips lowered and landscaped. The 50 hectares were transformed as part of the Cornish Heathlands Project which saw the brilliant-white mounds give way to purple heather and green gorse once some 20 million tonnes of spoil had been moved; the site was then opened to the public as a stunning viewpoint.

In February 2004 the Blackpool Trail was opened. This 1.5-mile wildlife trail now links the villages of Lanjeth, Foxhole and Old Pound, and skirts Blackpool Pit.

However, china clay villages such as Nanpean and Whitemoor have yet to see the benefits of the Cornish Heathlands Project, and concerns remain about the need to create new tips or reopen old workings so close to people's houses.

China Clay Museum

In the early 1950s the clay industry was being modernised and new production methods were being adopted. When the Cornish beam-pumping engine at Rostowrack china clay works was stopped, some people asked whether it could not be preserved in the St Austell district as a representative relic of Cornish engineering. An article in the *Cornish Guardian* debated the issue:

Apart from Rostowrack engine, others have ceased to be used, have been demolished or more carefully taken down during the last 12 to 14 years.

Could not some place be set aside in the china clay area for a museum at which the public could, at a small charge, see a permanent exhibition of bygones – not only ore engines but also other ancient and now out-moded industrial, social and domestic implements and machines?[4]

Perhaps with this were sown the seeds of what was to become Wheal Martyn China Clay Museum, established in 1974. This proved to be a popular attraction: throughout the 1970s and 1980s visitor numbers averaged 37,000 a year, and peaked at 60,000 in 1978. However, the museum's appeal declined during the 1990s as it fought to compete with a burgeoning range of new tourist attractions in the region.

Traffic and Roads

Traffic levels have risen dramatically in recent years, and the local roads were never designed to handle such a weight of traffic. What were once semi-rural

Wheal Martyn China Clay Museum, 1970s.

(IMERYS)

A winter's day at Holmbush, descending the hill towards Arch Garage, c.1930. (MR W. PAPPIN)

A rare glimpse of the old junction between Charlestown Road and Holmbush Road, c.1930. (MR W. PAPPIN)

The old junction between Charlestown Road and Holmbush Road, c.1930.
(MR W. PAPPIN)

Rural Holmbush during the 1960s, devoid of traffic and traffic lights. The Working Men's Institute in the middle distance was taken over by Marley Tiles, then Clemo's fruiterers. Tesco's supermarket was later built on the left. (MR R. DUTCH)

Road widening at Cuddra/Holmbush during the 1960s. Behind the lorries is Kellaway's Garage (a café in 2005) and the chimney stack of the clay dries. (MR R. DUTCH)

thoroughfares such as Holmbush Road and Daniel's Lane have become traffic-clogged arterial routes for heavy goods vehicles, locals and holiday-makers alike.

To cope with the influx of population and take the strain off the existing infrastructure, new roads were constructed during the 1960s. This was a period when modern was good and traditional was frowned upon, old buildings were sacrificed for road widening without too much thought being given to heritage or conservation:

The continuation of the widening of South Street, St Austell, started by the demolition of the old Corn Exchange, is to be considered by the County Highways Committee at their March meeting.[5]

This fine granite building adjoining the White Hart Hotel that had housed the library was demolished on 19 December 1960.

In 1957 South Street gained a new Inland Revenue building (when the new tax office was built in 1992 this became Cornwall House apartments). In the same year a new telephone exchange was built at East Hill, in an area called Paul's Square, where cottages once stood facing a cobbled yard with a tap in the middle.

In 1962 Trinity Street was created to link Truro

St Austell telephone exchange, Christmas 1952, with 'Jack and Jill' (Jack Blake and his colleague Jill).　　(Mr J. Blake)

A lost image of old St Austell: Burton Court that could be found behind the West Hill end of Fore Street until 1962.

(Mr R. Dutch)

This photograph was taken from the Odeon cinema during the early 1960s. Chandos Place was behind Fore Street. The rear of the New Inn can be seen, as well as Morgan Brothers' yard behind their shop, and Robins's Fish Bar.

(Mr R. Dutch)

The demolition of Phillips's Arcade in 1962 to make way for the construction of Trinity Street. Note Goodenough's shoe shop at the top of West Hill which was also lost at this time.
(Mr & Mrs F. Brewer)

Another view of the demolition, looking towards Fore Street.
(Mr & Mrs F. Brewer)

The scene from West Hill in 1962, looking towards the area that would become Sydney Grose's 'Roundabout' shop.
(Mr & Mrs F. Brewer)

Road and Bodmin Road with South Street. The maze of alley-ways and old houses behind Fore Street known as Chandos Place and Burton Place were also lost as the new town centre was created.

During the 1990s it was proposed that a new southern bypass and a north-eastern distributor road should be built. The first route was to run along the valley to the south of the existing bypass, across Charlestown Road and the railway track, and link up with the other road near Cuddra. However, vociferous campaigners under the banner of St Austell Road Action Group (STARAG) successfully defeated this proposal at the planning stage, leaving only the North Eastern Distributor Road to be built (the A391). This was completed on 20 January 1999, thus creating a new western boundary to the urban area.

The Eden Project

In 2000 the town was alive to 'The Big Build' – the transformation of a run-down china clay pit at Bodelva into the Eden Project. When the idea had originally been mooted a site near Roche had been considered. However, as the co-founders, Tim Smit and Jonathan Ball, developed the idea between 1994 and 1997, they found a fresh site, gained the Millennium Commission's landmark project funding and appointed the architects Nicholas Grimshaw to formulate a plan.

Between 15 May and 5 November 2000 the public was able to watch as two vast 'Biomes' were

Brochures were produced to advertise 'The Big Build' when the Eden Project was being built in 2000, as the public was encouraged to view the work being undertaken in the former clay pit at Bodelva.

constructed from over 800 huge steel hexagons to create a free-standing geodesic structure covering an area the size of 35 football pitches. While large pieces of earth-moving equipment appeared like toys from the rim of the 50 metre deep crater, and moved vast quantities of sand and soil, 'sky monkeys' abseiled

The Biomes of the Eden Project under construction on 20 July 2000, while extensive landscaping is being undertaken in the former china clay pit at Bodelva.

from the framework in order to glaze it with a thick plastic strong enough to support a rugby team. By the time the Eden Project opened, on 17 March 2001, over half a million people had already visited the site to see it being built. The Humid Tropics Biome, with its spectacularly large waterfall, was provided with some 1,000 species of tropical trees, plants and wildlife indigenous to the rainforest. Many had been propagated and stored at the former Watering Lane Nursery near Pentewan. Later birds were set free within its colossal dome. Complimenting this was the Warm Temperate Biome, hosting plants, fruit and flowers of the Mediterranean, South Africa and California. (For more about Eden today see pages 142–148.)

Hospitals

Another victim of change was St Austell Cottage Hospital. Originally paid for by public subscription and opened in 1919, the site is now being redeveloped for residential housing.

At least the town is blessed with St Austell Community (or Penrice) Hospital, which, rather ironically for a facility that included a maternity unit, had a rather laboured birth itself. A scheme for a new hospital in the area to cater for 150 patients was reported as early as 1950, but at that time no site had been chosen.[6] The plan was revived in 1954,[7] but it was not until June 1956 that approval to build at Porthpean was given,[8] after the site for the new hospital near the Duporth crossroads was generously provided by Mrs Cobbald Sawle. The hospital was eventually opened on 19 November 1964, while a subsequent extension was unveiled on 6 June 1973.

Development of the Town

In May 1958, townspeople were invited to see plans for a civic centre and new library, 'to be built in the field behind the present Rural District Council offices in Carlyon Road'.[9] However, such plans for this £100,000 development were not without their critics.[10] Despite this, Carlyon House and the library were built and still serve their respective functions in 2005, although the library may be relocated to the new town centre in the near future. Also, a new YMCA youth centre opened at Carlyon Road in June 1967.

In 1961 a model was displayed, 'of a heated swimming-pool which St Austell Urban Council

A view across St Austell, 1960s.

St Austell Hospital, 1934. (MRS G. GRIBBLE)

The nurses and staff of St Austell Hospital celebrating Christmas with a staff party, c.1952.
(MR R. DUTCH)

propose to build on the site of the projected Civic Centre at Carlyon Road...'[11] This eventually came to fruition, and Polkyth Leisure Centre was opened on 30 November 1974 with a large multi-purpose hall, squash courts, heated swimming-pool, bar and viewing areas. It has proved to be popular with many people, and several local leagues use this facility. Over the years it has also been a venue for a range of other activities, including visiting opera companies, motor bike shows, as well as sports tournaments. Just along the road, Trevarna old people's home was opened on 3 June 1983.

School Buildings

The town gained a new secondary school when Penrice School opened in January 1960 at the top of Charlestown Road. Poltair School was created in 1971, initially using West Hill School, before gradually taking over the eponymous Grammar School site. The buildings of West Hill School, familiar to so many St Austell people, and later used by St Austell College, disappeared during the 1990s; the sports field was replaced by a regional tax office, the school buildings by a housing development. Although not of any great architectural merit, the school was nonetheless a landmark in many old views of the town, as well as holding some affection with old pupils. The town has, however, gained more facilities for higher education. A new £171,000 block for St Austell Technical College in Palace Road was

completed in September 1967, while a new sixth-form college was built on the old cricket ground in Trevarthian Road in 1974, replacing the rather small sixth-form centre that had been tucked away in a corner of the Grammar School.

St Austell Foundry

At the foot of West Hill the buildings that comprised St Austell Foundry have largely disappeared. The

An aerial view of West Hill, St Austell, taken before the Second World War. West Hill School and the old St Austell Foundry buildings can be seen, but many of the other buildings and open spaces have long since disappeared. (Mr R. Sandercock)

A class of West Hill School, c.1954.   (Mr T. Allen)

West Hill School, looking down the footbridge that crossed Trinity Street, 1990s. The black building was a drama hall and the Portakabin on the left was a science lab. (Mr R. Sandercock)

West Hill School buildings, facing on to West Hill, 1990s. (Mr R. Sandercock)

West Hill School, prior to demolition, 1990s. In its final years it formed the West Hill Annexe of Cornwall College. (MR R. SANDERCOCK)

Cornish Mines Supplies at the foot of West Hill, seen here during the 1960s, provided materials for the building trade. In 2005 Mill Auto Supplies operate from these premises. (MR R. DUTCH)

Cornish Mines Supplies, 1960s. This old St Austell Foundry building was later demolished, along with the chimney stack.

site behind the former Cornish Mines Supplies building is used by Mill Auto Supplies in 2005. Across the road the old railway sheds and sidings of the Pentewan Railway have been swallowed up by a Co-op supermarket and car park.

The Beach

By the new millennium the Coliseum at Carlyon Bay, as well as the beach and car park, were a sorry sight. In 2003 plans were being drawn up for the demolition of the existing buildings and the construction of a beach-side development to include 511 luxury apartments, as well as a luxury 'boutique' hotel, shops and restaurants, a spa and pool (but, curiously, hardly any car parks). Johnny Sandelson, chief executive of The Ampersand Group, the property company behind this development to be known as The Beach, stated: 'We want to create something great for Cornwall, something new that can compete on the world stage'.[12] Many of the locals didn't see it that way; there were protests and a call for a public inquiry.[13]

With the £120 million project about to begin, on 4 January 2004 'Gossips' nightclub closed its doors for the last time, bringing 'the end of an era for an entertainments complex which has been a popular beach-side venue for generations of concert-goers and clubbers'.[14]

A promotional postcard for 'The Beach' at Carlyon Bay, 2004. The postcard is in the style of an old GWR poster used to advertise holidays in Cornwall.

(THE BEACH/ HEAVENLY MARKETING LTD)

Redevelopment of the Town Centre

In 2003 St Austell's much-criticised town centre, built around Aylmer Square in the mid-1960s, was demolished to make way for a new one. By the end of the year it was reported that: 'The largest town in Cornwall faces a New Year of unprecedented upheaval as a massive programme of redevelopment begins to forge ahead'.[15] This not only alluded to the town centre, but also to the following: the construction of the 'urban village' on the old railway goods' yard at Carlyon Road; the transformation of John Keay House – built in 1965 as ECLP's headquarters – into part of Cornwall College, along with the construction of an incongruous mould-green box on the front lawns which would be a new 300-seat theatre called The Keay (which opened in January 2005) costing £1.5 million; as well as the aforesaid complex at Carlyon Bay, described above.

During the early years of the twenty-first century, change has continued apace. The old art deco fire station inconveniently located on Bodmin Road was replaced with a new one at Carlyon Road in 2003. Similarly, the old Police Station at High Cross Street, having been replaced with a more modern building on the site of the Fairmead Hotel on the corner of Palace Road, was demolished to make way for, many believed, a hotel. At the time of writing the site is still vacant. A similar scheme was put forward by a London-based developer, and approved, for an 84-bedroomed hotel and restaurant on the cattle market at Pentewan Road. The cattle market had already been reduced in size by the construction of a ubiquitous McDonald's restaurant, providing an entirely new entrance to St Austell, as well as bringing to an end the centuries-old tradition of a true market town.

References
1 A.L. Rowse, *A Cornish Childhood*, p.220–223.
2 *Ibid.*, p.277.
3 *Cornish Guardian*, 17 August 1967, p.2.
4 *Cornish Guardian*, 21 June 1951, p.5.
5 *Cornish Guardian*, 2 February 1961, p.9.
6 *The St Austell Gazette & Cornwall County News*, 26 April 1950, p.5.
7 *Cornish Guardian*, 8 July 1954, p.3.
8 *Cornish Guardian*, 28 June 1956, p.9.
9 *Cornish Guardian*, 15 May 1958, p.9.
10 *Cornish Guardian*, 19 June 1958, p.8.
11 *Cornish Guardian*, 9 February 1961, p.3.
12 Quoted in an advertisement feature in *Beach Life*, p.27, a special supplement of *Country Life* magazine, summer 2003.
13 *Cornish Guardian*, 18 December 2003, p.15.
14 *Ibid.*
15 *Western Morning News*, 31 December 2003, p.46.

Cornwall Coliseum awaiting demolition on 19 December 2003, before the access road was widened in 2004.

By 2003 the swimming-pool had been full of sand for some time, and the whole complex was a sad shadow of its former self.

St Austell's regeneration scheme, 15 August 2003. The old town centre backing onto Trinity Street is being demolished.

The demolition of the railway goods' yard at Polkyth, ready for the site to be redeveloped as the Urban Village, photographed on 23 April 2003.

St Austell fire station, an art deco building that was built in 1939 and served the town until the fire station at Polkyth was opened in 2003. The building is pictured here in August 2004, facing an uncertain future.

The demolition of the old Police Station, 31 December 2002. The rear of the building is shown, with the old ECLP offices in the background. The workers discovered that large granite slabs formed the roof of the cells.

Chapter 11

Into a New Millennium

With painful irony, as the old cattle market site was being cleared, new perimeter signs appeared greeting motorists with 'Welcome to St Austell – Historic Market Town'. A defining feature had been consigned to the past. So what of the future, in the opening years of the twenty-first century? Of one thing we can be certain, the town and its hinterland are likely to change dramatically over the next few years. Under the headlines, 'Bright Outlook for St Austell', the *Cornish Guardian* announced on 21 April 2005, 'The future is looking bright for St Austell with almost £90 million set to be invested in and around the town over the next few years.'[1]

So what form will these investments take, and what will be the implications for the old market town?

Traditional Industries

It is hoped that the china clay industry will remain the mainstay of the local economy. Now in the hands of Imerys, the world's largest producer of china clay, the St Austell area still provides 39 per cent of the company's output and the 'white gold' is Britain's largest bulk export, being sent to more than a hundred countries. Investment continues – some £27 million will be provided in 2005, and the staggering range of uses for this innocuous material continues to grow beyond its traditional uses in porcelain, paper, paint, rubber and plastic.[2]

Developments at the Eden Project

Building on its success, a new Education Centre is currently under construction, dubbed Big Build 2. Aiming to centralise resources, the new facility is due to open in the summer of 2005. It was designed by the architects Nicholas Grimshaw & Partners and was inspired by a plant form. Tim Smit, Eden's chief executive, was excited about the design and said, '... I guarantee [it] will be the most photographed and loved building of 2005.'[3] The ground floor will be used for exhibitions and workshops, the first floor

Hidden within a 60-metre deep 10-hectare former china clay pit and surrounded by a dramatic horticultural landscape, Eden is home to the two largest conservatories (Biomes) in the world. The entire site covers 50 hectares. Opened to the public in March 2001, it is a 'Living Theatre of People and Plants' dedicated to the appreciation and study of human dependence on plants.

RICHARD KALINA

The Humid Tropics Biome lets visitors experience the sights, smells and sheer scale of the rainforest in the world's largest greenhouse. The Warm Temperate Biome features the climes of South Africa, California and the Mediterranean and enables visitors to walk amongst the orange and lemon trees, olive groves and gnarled vines. In the crescent-shaped terraces of the Outdoor Landscape, the story of plants that have changed the world and which could change the future is told.

RICHARD KALINA

The Biomes comprise a two-layer steel curved space frame, the hex-tri-hex, with an outer layer of hexagons (the largest of which is 11 metres across), plus the occasional pentagon and an inner layer of hexagons and triangles – all bolted together like a giant Meccano kit.

MARC HILL

Eden's new Education Centre represents an inspired way of learning. This inspirational hub will host events, exhibitions and education for all. An exhibit in its own right, it was inspired by natural form, is crafted from natural materials and is dedicated to the plant engine that powers our world. Eden got its inspiration from plant architecture. After all, it does have a 400-million-year-old track record.

CHRIS SAVILLE

The Biomes contain thousands of plants from around the world – some common and some rare – collected from botanic gardens, research collections and private individuals or commercial nurseries. Many of the plants arrived as seeds or cuttings and were (and are still) grown at Eden's own nurseries.

TOP PICTURE: BOB PERRY
LEFT: RICHARD KALINA
BOTTOM: TOM SMITH

Eden Live is Eden's events programme, which incorporates music, performance, workshops and talks based around specific themes each year. Eden's outdoor arena, with a capacity of around 5,000, has played host to a diverse range of events, including the BBC's 'Songs of Praise' and 'Last Night of the Proms', as well as the Eden Sessions. The latter have featured international artists such as Moby, Pulp, Brian Wilson, P.J. Harvey, Badly Drawn Boy and Air (pictured) and have also hosted world music artists through music partner WOMAD.

will provide space for school groups, while refreshments will be available on the second floor, which will also include more space for exhibitions.

Funding for this new phase of development has come from a £10 million grant from the Millennium Commission, as well as £2.89 million from the South West Regional Development Agency. A new desert Biome is also in the early planning stage.

Access to Eden

Two trails for horse riders and walkers have been opened up recently. A four-mile trail from Bugle to the Eden Project traverses the heathland of Treskilling Downs, while a five-mile-long route reaches the Eden Project from Wheal Martyn through the Clay Country near the landmark 'white pyramid' of Great Treverbyn sky tip. The cost of these devel-

Designed by Paul Bonomini, the WEEE Man, is a huge robotic figure (weighing 3.3 tonnes, he is 7 metres tall) made from the amount of waste electrical and electronic products that an average UK citizen will throw away in his or her lifetime, according to current rates. At the time of writing most of these products go straight into landfill. From January 2006 manufactures and retailers will be responsible for recycling this waste under new EU legislation called the WEEE (Waste Electrical and Electronic Equipment) Directive. BEN FOSTER

The new bridge constructed over Bodmin Road near Ruddlemoor to carry the trail between Wheal Martyn and the Eden Project. The paths themselves were still under construction at the time the picture was taken on 1 May 2005.

Eden's popularity has led to the site now employing several hundred full-time staff – 95 per cent of whom come from the local area. A new Education Centre, additional covered areas and a third Biome (Dry Tropics) are currently under construction. APEX

Eden's Biomes take on a supernatural appearance in front of a sea of tulips, seen here on 30 March 2005. A million bulbs were planted for the Bulb Mania season.

The Humid Tropics Biome at the Eden Project, photographed on 30 March 2005, shows how the trees and shrubs are beginning to mature into an authentic jungle.

The landscape around the Humid Tropics Biomes is softened by the new growth of spring, 30 April 2005.

opments was met by lottery funds through the joint involvement of Active England, Imerys and the Eden Project. Meanwhile, Restormel Borough Council has been creating a footpath linking Par Beach to Eden. Plans continue to be considered for a new road link from the A391 to the A30 Link Road, with no less than nine different variations of route under review.

Increased awareness of the area can of course be attributed to the Eden Project and other noteworthy local gardens.

The Lost Gardens of Heligan

The house and gardens at Heligan were owned by the Tremayne family from the late-sixteenth century until the time of the First World War. Over the years they created an extraordinary garden that became home to many exotic new plants from overseas and introduced new horticultural techniques that came about during the Victorian era. The gardens were also very special as the family had developed a model farm that made the estate almost totally self-sufficient.[4]

During the twentieth century the gardens were considered 'lost', as they were abandoned at the end of the First World War. That was until Tim Smit and John Nelson, who would later co-found the Eden Project, along with John Willis who had inherited the grounds through the Tremayne family, stumbled into them on 16 February 1990. With the help of a team of volunteers they revealed beneath a jungle of brambles and self-seeded sycamores, not just the original garden format, but many of the old ornamental shrubs. Like latter-day explorers they unearthed the old greenhouses, gardeners' quarters, the walled gardens, pineapple pits and summer-house. Gradually each section was brought back to life, old varieties of vegetables were re-introduced, and after much experimentation pineapples were once again grown – one of the first successful fruits being sent to Her Majesty the Queen.

Now, at each turn, a fresh glimpse of our past is revealed. How a regular supply of fresh flowers were grown for Lady Tremayne, how the food was produced for the table, fertilised by the 'night soil' from the house, where the family would have frolicked in the Crystal Grotto, or rode out through the woods beyond The Jungle. Hugely popular with visitors, it is little wonder that the grounds at Heligan have been voted the nation's favourite gardens.

Pine Lodge, Boscundle

Pine Lodge is a 30-acre site developed by Ray and Shirley Clemo, who transformed it into delightful gardens and introduced some 6,000 species of plants, trees and flowers from all over the world. It includes an arboretum, pinetum, and Japanese garden.

The Moor Cottage Development

In April 2005 plans were presented for the transformation of Moor Cottage (called The White House by the developers) near Tregorrick into a four star luxury hotel and spa. This site had once been the home of the Coode family, but had been neglected for over 50 years. As a result of the success of the Eden Project and the Lost Gardens of Heligan there appears to be a need for a top level hotel in the area. Plans for a similar establishment at Scredda, to the north-east of the town, were turned down. Developers, CMR Leisure of Bristol, propose to invest £20 million in this secluded 38-acre site that is within walking distance of the town, yet close to the major tourist attractions. The old house would be restored, and 56 bedrooms created in an extension to the rear, while the stable block would be transformed into a sauna, swimming-pool and gym. Some 60 lodges arranged in a crescent-shape would be constructed in the grounds, to provide self-catering

Moor Cottage, 15 April 2005. Empty for many years, and virtually out of sight in its wooded grounds, it now awaits revitalisation as a possible hotel and spa complex.

Pochin House, Carclaze, 24 April 2005, created from old Carclaze clay dry. The process was not without its difficulties, including reducing the height of the old chimney and stabilising the building's foundations before it could be turned into two and three-bedroomed apartments.

and timeshare accommodation. The plans also include conference and function rooms which, like the pool and spa, should be available to outside groups as well as guests.

It is hoped that the scheme will provide up to 240 full- and part-time jobs. The developers have vowed to restore the run-down gardens and revitalise the lakes in the grounds which, over the years, have silted up and become overgrown with reeds and willow trees.[5]

The Urban Village

The old railway goods' depot has been developed into a residential housing and shopping area of some considerable size. A new road layout has been created, including the creation of a new roundabout at its entrance onto the existing junction of Carlyon Road and Tremayne Place.

A second phase of the Urban Village off Carlyon Road is being planned at the time of writing, which

The Urban Village, still under construction on 30 April 2005, will add Polkyth Parade and Trevail Way to the local map. The building on the left will form shops with flats above.

Another view of the Urban Village on 30 April 2005, taken from the same vantage point as the photograph on page 140.

will include another 20 starter homes designed for shared ownership or rent when the old council depot is developed. On completion the scheme at the former goods' yard will include a village green, shops and offices, as well as 147 new homes, costing more than £18 million.

Developments at Polkyth Leisure Centre

Now over 30 years old, the leisure centre has needed to be upgraded for some time. As well as a recent refurbishment, plans have been made for a new fitness suite, dance studio and conference room, while the pool will see flumes and other water features added.

Aldi Stores Ltd

The former garage premises of Cundy, Phillips & Geake, UBM, and more recently Cornish Ford and Vospers, at the foot of Slades Road has been demolished in 2005 to make way for another supermarket. Aldi Stores Ltd is to be constructed on this site. Large sections of pre-cast concrete are being utilised, reducing the build time.

St Austell Hospital

A development of 34 houses and apartments is being built on the site of the former St Austell Hospital. The main hospital building has been retained to form a house conversion (and temporary site office), while all other buildings within the grounds have been removed. Named Edgcumbe Rise, the scheme will comprise three-, four-, and five-bedroomed detached houses as well as two-bedroomed apartments, many of which should enjoy glorious views over the town.

Moorland Road clinic has also closed in 2005, with community nursing having been transferred to Penrice Hospital.

Charlestown Foundry Site

The former Charlestown Engineering premises, along with other parcels of land within the village of Charlestown, was purchased by Wainhomes in 2004. This company has proposed to build 160 to 190 houses on the land once occupied by the busy foundry. The foundry had an illustrious history of providing equipment for the china clay industry, as well as producing vital equipment for the war effort during the Second World War. This included

Aldi Stores Ltd under construction at the junction between Slades Road and Sandy Hill on 15 April 2005. New concrete floors are being poured.

Charlestown Engineering's premises, 15 April 2005. The Machine Shop is on the left, the more recently constructed office block is on the right.

The sensitive nature of the site can be appreciated in this photograph, which clearly illustrates the close proximity of the large area to be redeveloped to the church and existing cottages.

The once busy foundry was the first place that people saw on decending the hill to Charlestown, and was an integral part of this working village, with its harbour, estate cottages and a wide range of businesses.

components for the Mulberry Harbour landing stages that were so important during the D-Day invasion in Normandy in June 1944.

The new development is also set to include industrial units as well as social amenities for community use. Some of the old historic features including the brick Machine Shop that faces the road and the water wheel look set to be retained.

To the south of the churchyard, the old Hooper's Yard is being used for 13 new houses.

Meanwhile a bid is being made to gain World Heritage status for Charlestown, as well as the Luxulyan Valley, but a decision on this will not be promulgated until June 2006.

The College Sites

The transfer of Cornwall College, St Austell, including the Sixth Form College, to John Keay House, has left a surplus of educational facilities in the area between St Austell Brewery and Palace Road. At the time of writing tentative proposals are being put forward to demolish the existing buildings to make way for a residential development of 200 to 235 houses on the site, as well as office blocks opposite the Brewery. Methleigh House, part of the college campus facing Palace Road, is not considered suitable for conversion to residential use, so is also earmarked for conversion into offices.

Meanwhile, a proposal has been made to create 53 more dwellings on surplus land adjacent to John Keay House, at Lewis Way and the old Endeavour Club, while the Sedgemoor building in Priory Road is being converted into 4,330 square metres of office space. In October 2005 this building will see the arrival of 400 staff from Cornwall County Council and the Central Cornwall Primary Care Trust, the former moving from Penwinnick House and Carlyon Road, the latter vacating their John Keay House offices.

Duporth Holiday Village

At the time of writing, a Draft Development Brief has been prepared for Duporth Holiday Village. The present use is no longer viable, so it is proposed to use the available land primarily for new housing. The site covers some 44 acres, but taking out the substantial areas of mature woodland, approximately 21 acres can be developed. At the moment Government policy requires that new properties built on previously developed land (brown field sites) should be built at a density of not less than 30 units per hectare. So, depending on the type and size of the houses, this could result in some 300 dwellings being built. (This compares with approximately 60 houses in the existing estate to the east, and about 25 dwellings in the residential area to the west). They would probably range from one- and two-

bedroomed apartments to four-bedroomed houses. The current proposals would retain some of the existing old buildings and the squat clock tower with its cupola. Offices, craft workshops and a café may also be built on the site.

To cope with the increased traffic that would inevitably be created, a new primary access road could be developed on Duporth Road (Brick Hill), the present main drive being restricted to emergency use and access for immediate residents. Traffic calming measures would also be put in place along Duporth Road in a bid to reduce traffic flow, possibly by narrowing the carriageway to one lane. The junctions with Duporth Road and Porthpean Road, and Porthpean Road onto the A390 would also need to be improved, possibly by installing traffic lights.

Whether these proposals come to fruition remains to be seen. Certainly the Duporth area is likely to see substantial changes in the next few years.

The Future

The rate of change in St Austell and outlying districts is at present staggering, and with so many developments occurring in a wide range of places, the changes are often difficult to keep up with. Pessimists may be dismayed and say that the old town and old ways have gone for ever; optimists will argue that residents face an exciting future. Perhaps people felt the same way when the railway arrived in the 1850s. Only future generations will be able to reflect on which group was right.

References
[1] *Cornish Guardian*, 21 April 2005, p.1.
[2] *Western Morning News*, 13 April 2005, p.43.
[3] Quoted in internet press release (http://www.eden-project.com/5698.htm).
[4] Details found on Lost Gardens of Heligan website (http://www.heligan.com).
[5] *Western Morning News*, 15 April 2005, p.29.

Par Moor Motor Museum has been under construction for some time on what was once farm land. An opening date has not yet been published. Beyond it is the main railway line and golf course.

Progress on The Beach, showing the controversial sea defences, 1 May 2005.

A forlorn Crinnis Beach, 1 May 2005.

Cypress Avenue, Carlyon Bay. During the spring of 2005 the two rows of cypress firs that had been part of the scene for so long were felled. Amongst the trees on the right and behind the golf range can be seen Imerys' office block. A hotel may be built on the open land in the foreground in the near future. This photograph was taken on 1 May 2005.

Wheal Regent Park, part of the Crinnis Wood development, has been built amongst the fir trees and old mine workings at Carlyon Bay. It is seen here on 1 May 2005.

An advertisement for Carlyon Bay Garages, 1995. Less than ten years later the business was gone, the site redeveloped with houses so that no evidence of it remains.

Bibliography

Books

Bainbridge, George. *The Wooden Ships and the Iron Men of the Cornish China Clay Trade* (Charlestown Estates Ltd., 1980)

Barton, D.B. *A Historical Survey of The Mines and Mineral Railways of East Cornwall and West Devon* (D. Barton, 1964)

Brokenshire, Valerie. *The Archive Photographs Series St Austell* (Chalford Publishing, 1997)

Bunn, Cyril. *The Book of St Austell – The Story of a China Clay Town* (Barracuda Books Ltd, 1978)

Collins, David and Jeremy Jackson. *St Austell Speedway* (J & S Publications, 1998)

Hammond, Canon Joseph. *A Cornish Parish: Being an Account of St Austell, Town, Church, District and People* (Skeffington & Son, 1897)

Hamilton Jenkin, A.K. *Mines and Miners of Cornwall – VIII. Truro to the Clay District* (Truro Bookshop, 1964).

Hancock, Peter. *Cornwall at War* (Halsgrove, 2002)

Hancock, Peter. *St Austell – The Golden Years* (Halsgrove, 2004)

Hudson, Kenneth. *The History of English China Clays – Fifty Years of Pioneering Growth* (David & Charles, 1968)

Larn, Richard and Bridget. *Charlestown: The History of a Cornish Seaport* (Richard and Bridget Larn, 1994)

Lewis, M.J.T. *The Pentewan Railway 1829–1918* (D.B. Barton, 1960)

Luck, Liz. *Brewing for Cornwall – A Family Tradition   The Story of St Austell Brewery 1851–2001* (St Austell Brewery Ltd, 2001)

Murray, John. *A Handbook for Travellers in Devon and Cornwall (1859)* (David & Charles Reprints, 1971)

Penderill-Church, John. *The China Clay Industry and Industrial Relations* (John Penderill-Church, 1980)

Rowse, A.L. *A Cornish Childhood* (Jonathan Cape, 1942)

Smith, Archie. *Uphill All the Way* (Camomile Press, 1994)

Stallworthy, Dave and Tony Lethbridge. *The Story of Grass Track & Speedway in Cornwall Featuring St Austell Speedway* (Dave Stallworthy and Tony Lethbridge)

Stockdale, F.W.L. *Excursions in the County of Cornwall* (Simkin and Marshall, *1824)*

Tangye, Nigel. *Cornwall Newspapers – Eighteenth & Nineteenth Century* (The Trevithick Society, 1980)

Tregellas, Walter H. *Tourist Guide to Cornwall and the Scilly Isles* (Edward Stanford, 1891)

Directories

Kelly's *Directory of Cornwall* (editions from 1897, 1893, 1923, 1927 and 1935)

Pigot's *Directory of Devon and Cornwall*, 1830

Slater's *Directory of Cornwall* (editions from 1852 and 1853)

Booklets

Hockin, Clifford. *St Austell Brewery – Established 1851*

Quality of Life Report 2003 (Restormel Borough Council, 2003)

Pamphlets

Bowditch, Ivor. *The Essential Component* (Imerys Minerals Ltd, 2001)

Blueprint for Cornwall 2003 (Imerys Minerals Ltd, 2003)

Newspapers

Cornish Guardian

Cornwall County News

Mid Cornwall Advertiser

Royal Cornwall Gazette

St Austell Gazette

West Briton

Western Morning News

Subscribers

Kathleen Alexander, St Austell

Joy Andrew, Boscoppa Farm, St Austell, Cornwall

Noreen and Derek Atkinson, Gorran Haven, St Austell

D.E. Baker, St Austell, Cornwall

Lewis J. Baker

M. and J. Bassett, St Austell

Charles Rex Bate, Bugle, St Austell, Cornwall

Fernley Bate (In Memory of), St Blazey Gate

Wilfred E. Bawden, St Austell, Cornwall

R.J. Beal

Janet and David Bell, St Austell

M. and J. Bennett, St Austell

George Bennetto, St Austell, Cornwall

Ken and Violet Best, St Austell, Cornwall

Frederick David Blake

Jack and Grace Blake, St Austell, Cornwall

Evril D. Bray (Currian), St Austell

M.W. Brewer, Whitemoor

Rex Brewer, Duporth, St Austell

John Britton, Pinhoe, Exeter

Mrs Y. Burge, St Austell

Dr Elizabeth A. Burroughs (née Clyma), St Austell

K.J. Burrow, Bucks Cross, Devon

Martin Burt, St Austell, Cornwall

Glynis Butler-Lee, St Austell, Cornwall

Mr and Mrs N.J. Carter, St Austell, Cornwall

Mr William H. Champion, Polgooth

P.A. Chantry, St Austell

Ada R. Chard (née Davis), St Austell, Cornwall

Charlestown Post Office, Adrian Burley

Zak Chenoweth, St Austell

Margaret Clemow, St Austell

James Arthur Cocks, St Austell, Cornwall

I.M. Coleman, Sticker

Barbara Cook, Tregrehan Mills

Geoff Cornelius

Mrs Shirley A. Craddock, St Austell, Cornwall

Tony Cross, St Austell

Ann Cundy, Coombe, St Austell

Marjorie E. Davey, St Austell

Norman R. Dawe, St Austell

Christopher J. Dew, St Austell, Cornwall

Heather R. Double, St Austell, Cornwall

Michael Dowrick, St Austell, Cornwall

Stephen K. Dowrick, St Stephen, St Austell

Deidre and Reg Drew, St Austell

Des Durant, St Austell, Cornwall

David and Jane Durnford, Penwithick, St Austell

Kevin and Vanessa Dyer, St Austell, Cornwall

Pamela J. Ellis, Trewoon, St Austell, Cornwall

Robert and Shirley Evans, Pentewan, Cornwall

P.R. Evely, son of Polgooth, and true Trelawney man

Ann Ford, St Austell, Cornwall

Mrs Jillian Ford, St Austell

Lynne M. Ford, and Lynne M. and Megan L. Trudgeon, St Austell

Mr P.M.J. Foster, St Austell, Cornwall

Robert M. Foster, Trewoon, St Austell

R.P. Francis, Pentewan, St Austell

Mrs Edna Frost, St Austell, Cornwall. Age 100 on 25.04.05.

Mr M.P. Garfield, Carbis Moor, St Austell

Mr Jack Gates, Queensland, Australia

Marie and Ian Gayton, Roche, St Austell

Mrs Alma Geach

William Trevor Geach, St Dennis, St Austell, Cornwall

W. Keith George, St Austell, Cornwall

Victoria and Colin Gilbert, Exeter, Devon

P.W. John Giles, St Austell, Cornwall

Edward S.J. Golley, St Austell, Cornwall

Simon P. Golley, St Austell, Cornwall

David Goss and Marta Barron Lopez, Getxo, Bizkaia, Spain

Dr Jonathan and Sarah Goss, Choppington, Northumberland

Sidney and Primrose Goss, St Austell, Cornwall

Kevin and Stephanie Gray-Roberts, Caerhayes, Cornwall

Mr and Mrs D.J. Green, St Austell, Cornwall

Mr Jeffrey Green, Stenalees, St Austell, Cornwall

Geoffrey E. Gregory, Trewoon, Cornwall

Barry Grime, St Austell

Mr Howard Grose, Slades Supply Stores

Mrs D. Guest, St Austell

Haley, St Austell

Mrs Connie A. Hancock

David J. Hancock

Wesley and Lorna Hancock, Penwithick

Alan Harris, Lanivet, Cornwall

G.W. and D. Harris, Porthpean, Cornwall
Jack and Jessica Harvey, St Austell
The Harvey Family, St Austell, Cornwall
Marjorie I.J. Hawke, St Austell, Cornwall
Russell and Beattie Hawke, Fowey, Cornwall
Joe Hawkins, St Austell, Cornwall
Peter Heayns, St Austell, Cornwall
L.A. Hendy, St Austell, Cornwall
Mrs V.M. Hendy, Charlestown
Mr L.C. Herne, St Austell, Cornwall
Stanley Hibbard, St Austell, Cornwall
J.E. Hickling, St Austell
Eldred Hicks, Penwithick, St Austell
Richard and Julie Hobba, St Austell, Cornwall
Mr W.J. Hobba, Charlestown, St Austell
Michael J. Hocking,
T. Roy Hocking, St Austell, Cornwall
Dave and Sally Hodge, Penwithick, St Austell
Terry, Marcia and Matthew Hodge, St Austell
Roy Holland, Style Glaze, St Austell
Mr and Mrs D. Honey, St Austell, Cornwall
Derek Hooper, Old Pound, Nanpean
John Hooper, St Austell, Cornwall
M.J. Hooper, Tavistock, Devon
C. Hoskin, St Austell, Cornwall
Henry and Heather Hughes, Summercourt,
  Newquay
Mr and Mrs D. Huitson, St Austell
Maurice and Christine Hunkin, Trewoon
Thomas Barry Hunkin, Tregiskey Farm
Mr G. Husband and Family (in memory of
  Moosey Husband), St Austell
Jenefer and Norman Husband, St Austell,
  Cornwall
Rob and Ros Husband, St Stephen
Tony Isaacs, St Austell, Cornwall
Jeremy Jackson
Mrs B.V.H. James, St Austell
Mrs Margaret A. James, Bugle
Mrs I.A. Jeffery (née Swiggs), St Austell
Hilda N. Jenkin
Fay B.A. Jepson, St Austell, Cornwall
Sylvia I. Johns, High Street, St Austell,
  Cornwall
Mr and Mrs R. Jones
Gordon Joslin, St Austell, Cornwall
Mr Bernard J.A. Kellaway
L. Gordon Kellow, St Dennis
David M. Kent
Richard and Sheila Kent, St Austell, Cornwall
Eric J. Knowles, St Austell, Cornwall
T.D. Knowles, St Austell, Cornwall
J. Lander, St Austell, Cornwall
Bryan A. Lansdell, St Austell, Cornwall

Mr Tony Larcombe, St Austell, Cornwall
Mike Lean, Victoria, Roche
Penny Lean, Manchester
L. Lee, Penwithick, St Austell
Betty Liddicoat, widow of Phil, boat builder,
  St Austell
Mrs Ivy Liddicoat, St Austell
Mr and Mrs N. Liddicoat, Mevagissey,
  Cornwall
Mrs Norma and Miss Sharon Lobb
Angela J. Macey, Foxhole, St Austell
Mr M.J. Mantell, St Dennis, St Austell,
  Cornwall
Hugo Manuell, Burngullow, St Austell,
  Cornwall
Sandra M. Marks, St Austell, Cornwall
Peter Marriott, Mevagissey
Mrs C.L. Martin, Trewoon, St Austell
S.L. Mears and M.J. Truscott, Trethurgy,
  St Austell
Jennifer A. Michael, St Austell, Cornwall
Kerrie Michael, St Austell, Cornwall
Michael G. Michell, St Austell, Cornwall
Jim Mitchell, Slades, St Austell
Arthur Moon
M.Y. Moon, British Consulate, Toronto, Canada
Michael Anthony Mugford, St Austell,
  Cornwall
Frances Murfitt (née Gilbert), St Austell,
  Cornwall
Douglas Murphy, Bugle, St Austell
Miss Elizabeth Nagy, Towan
Sarah Nelson, St Austell, Cornwall
Graeme J. Netherton, Keynsham, Bristol
Kenneth H. Netherton, St Blazey, Cornwall
Mrs Ellen Neville, St Austell, Cornwall
Ken Newcombe, St Austell
Andrew Northam, St Austell, Cornwall
Maurice and June Opie, St Austell, Cornwall
Chris Osborne, St Austell
Murray Owen, St Austell, Cornwall
David and June Parnell
Roger Parnell, St Austell, Cornwall
Barry Pearce, St Austell
Crystal and Graham Pearce, St Austell
Lawson Pearce, St Austell
Marian J. Pearce
W. Pearse, Sandy Hill, St Austell
W.T. Pearse, Huntingdon, Cambridgeshire
Geoffrey Keith Penhaligon
Mrs Susan A. Penhaligon, Trewoon, St Austell
Queenie I. Penhaligon, St Austell, Cornwall
Jenefer Leathlean Penhall, Newton Abbot,
  Devon

Judith A. Portsmouth, Trowbridge, Wiltshire
Sylvia J. Powlesland, Polgooth
D.V. Priston, St Austell, Cornwall
Sharon A. Raggett, St Austell, Cornwall
Phil Ratty
Gareth Stephen Redington, St Austell, Cornwall
Helen Louise Redington, St Austell, Cornwall
Stephen Redington, St Austell, Cornwall
Susan P. Redington, St Austell, Cornwall
Chris and Marie Reynolds, Penwithick, St Austell
Natasha and Sophie Rice-Payton
Carol Richards, St Austell
Mark A. Richards, Carn Grey, St Austell, Cornwall
Paul Richards, St Austell
Joyce Rideout, St Blazey, Cornwall
Dr Mark and Mrs Heidi Roberts, Histon, Cambridge
Dorothy Rosevear, St Austell, Cornwall
R.J. Rosevear, St Austell, Cornwall
Martin A. Rouse, St Austell, Cornwall
Martin John Rowe, St Ives, Cambridgeshire
Brian Rowe, Sticker, St Austell
Edna and Derek Rowe, St Austell
Roy (Tiny) Rowe, St Austell, Cornwall
Mrs V.J. Rowe, St Austell, Cornwall
Glyn Rowett, St Austell, Cornwall
Mr C.S. Rowse, St Austell
Mr Derek K. Rowse, St Austell, Cornwall
Jackie and Mark Rudge, Porthpean, St Austell, Cornwall
Mrs E. Rundle (née Endean), St Austell
F.A. Rundle, Penwithick, St Austell
T. Desmond. T. Rundle, Westbury, Wiltshire
Andrew Russell, North Carolina, USA
Alison Schwab, Charlestown, St Austell, Cornwall
S.H. Seccombe
Darren M. Seed, St Austell
Teresa Slater (née Barrett), St Austell, Cornwall
Miss C. Sleeman, St Austell
Owen Sleeman, Rocks Pit, Bugle, Cornwall
Archie Smith, Gorran Haven
Cleon Smith, Bugle, St Austell
Frederick Ronald Squires, St Austell, Cornwall
St Austell Brewery Co Ltd,
Barry and Connie Stark, New Jersey, USA
Brian Stephens, Tregonissey, St Austell
Ken Stone, St Austell
Mr John Strong
Victoria Studley, St Austell, Cornwall
Rosemary Sutton, St Austell, Cornwall

Brian M. Sweet, St Stephen-in-Brannel
John Sweet, Polgooth, St Austell
Monty N. Swiggs, St Austell
Mrs Joy V. Tamblyn, St Austell, Cornwall
Mr A.C. Tancock, St Austell
Edith and Peter Taylor, Nanpean, St Austell
Miss Madison Tellam, Trethowel, St Austell, Cornwall
Pamela J. Ternouth, St Austell
Hazel Tippett, St Austell, Cornwall
Brenda Tomkies-Smith, Quendon, Essex
George A. Tomkies, Gunnislake, Cornwall
Maureen Tomkies-Scott, Gorran Haven, Cornwall
Alan Toms, St Austell
M. Toms, Foxhole, St Austell, Cornwall
Mr and Mrs G. Tonkin, Albury, New South Wales, Australia
W. John Tonkin, formerly of Bugle
Rodney S. Trembeth, St Austell
Mrs J.M. Trudgeon, St Stephen, Cornwall
Colin and Elizabeth Trudgian, Par
Mrs Jennifer Trudgian, Sticker
David A. Tucker, St Austell, Cornwall
R.E. Turner, Lower Sticker, St Austell
Hazel Lousia Vian, St Austell, Cornwall
S.G. Vincent, St Austell, Cornwall
Sheila and John (Joe) Vivian, St Austell
Michael Voyce, St Austell
Miss Coleen Walker, St Austell, Cornwall
Mrs Jean Maureen Walker, Widnes, Cheshire
John F.W. Walling, Newton Abbot, Devon
Cuntelleran Brewyon, Malcolm F. Waters, St Austell
Mr and Mrs R. Webb, St Stephen, Cornwall
Mrs H. Wenmouth, St Austell, Cornwall
Mr K.B. Westaway, St Austell, Cornwall
Graham Wherry, St Stephen-in-Brannel, Cornwall
The White Family, Carlyon Bay, St Austell
C.N. Wiblin, St Levan, Cornwall
The Wilkins Family, Tregrehan, St Austell
Anthony A. Wilkinson
Mrs Barbara Williams (née Stone), Beech Road, St Austell
Christopher J. Williams, Bethel, St Austell
Elizabeth Williams and Stuart Roberts, St Austell, Cornwall
Mrs Jean Wilshaw, Roche, St Austell
Miss Lorna A. Wilson, St Austell, Cornwall
D. and P.J. Withe, Colbiggan
Harry Woodhouse, Porthpean
Stella and David Wright, Roche, St Austell
P.S. Yates, formerly of Roche Road, Bugle

Community Histories

The Book of Addiscombe • Canning and Clyde Road
Residents Association and Friends
The Book of Addiscombe, Vol. II • Canning and Clyde Road
Residents Association and Friends
The Book of Ashburton • Stuart Hands and Pete Webb
The Book of Axminster with Kilmington • Les Berry
and Gerald Gosling
The Book of Bakewell • Trevor Brighton
The Book of Bampton • Caroline Seward
The Book of Barnstaple • Avril Stone
The Book of Barnstaple, Vol. II • Avril Stone
The Book of The Bedwyns • Bedwyn History Society
The Book of Bergh Apton • Geoffrey I. Kelly
The Book of Bickington • Stuart Hands
The Book of Bideford • Peter Christie and Alison Grant
Blandford Forum: A Millennium Portrait • Blandford Forum
Town Council
The Book of Boscastle • Rod and Anne Knight
The Book of Bourton-on-the-Hill, Batsford and Sezincote •
Allen Firth
The Book of Bramford • Bramford Local History Group
The Book of Breage & Germoe • Stephen Polglase
The Book of Bridestowe • D. Richard Cann
The Book of Bridport • Rodney Legg
The Book of Brixham • Frank Pearce
The Book of Buckfastleigh • Sandra Coleman
The Book of Buckland Monachorum & Yelverton •
Pauline Hamilton-Leggett
The Book of Budleigh Salterton • D. Richard Cann
The Book of Carharrack • Carharrack Old
Cornwall Society
The Book of Carshalton • Stella Wilks and Gordon
Rookledge
The Parish Book of Cerne Abbas • Vivian and
Patricia Vale
The Book of Chagford • Iain Rice
The Book of Chapel-en-le-Frith • Mike Smith
*The Book of Chittlehamholt with
Warkleigh & Satterleigh* • Richard Lethbridge
The Book of Chittlehampton • Various
The Book of Codford • Romy Wyeth
The Book of Colney Heath • Bryan Lilley
The Book of Constantine • Moore and Trethowan
The Book of Cornwood and Lutton • Compiled by
the People of the Parish

The Book of Crediton • John Heal
The Book of Creech St Michael • June Small
The Book of Crowcombe, Bicknoller and Sampford Brett •
Maurice and Joyce Chidgey
The Book of Crudwell • Tony Pain
The Book of Cullompton • Compiled by the People
of the Parish
The Book of Dawlish • Frank Pearce
*The Book of Dulverton, Brushford,
Bury & Exebridge* • Dulverton and District Civic Society
The Book of Dunster • Hilary Binding
The Book of Easton • Easton Village History Project
The Book of Edale • Gordon Miller
The Ellacombe Book • Sydney R. Langmead
The Book of Exmouth • W.H. Pascoe
The Book of Grampound with Creed • Bane and Oliver
The Book of Gosport • Lesley Burton and
Brian Musselwhite
The Book of Haughley • Howard Stephens
The Book of Hayle • Harry Pascoe
The Book of Hayling Island & Langstone • Peter Rogers
The Book of Helston • Jenkin with Carter
The Book of Hemyock • Clist and Dracott
The Book of Herne Hill • Patricia Jenkyns
The Book of Hethersett • Hethersett Society
Research Group
The Book of High Bickington • Avril Stone
The Book of Honiton • Gerald Gosling
The Book of Ilsington • Dick Wills
The Book of Kingskerswell • Carsewella Local
History Group
The Book of Lamerton • Ann Cole and Friends
Lanner, A Cornish Mining Parish • Sharron
Schwartz and Roger Parker
The Book of Leigh & Bransford • Malcolm Scott
The Second Book of Leigh & Bransford • Malcolm Scott
The Book of Litcham with Lexham & Mileham • Litcham
Historical and Amenity Society
The Book of Llangain • Haydyn Williams
The Book of Loddiswell • Loddiswell Parish History Group
The New Book of Lostwithiel • Barbara Fraser
The Book of Lulworth • Rodney Legg
The Book of Lustleigh • Joe Crowdy
The Book of Lydford • Compiled by Barbara Weeks
The Book of Lyme Regis • Rodney Legg
The Book of Manaton • Compiled by the People
of the Parish

For details of any of the above titles or if you are interested in writing your own history, please contact: Commissioning Editor, Community Histories, Halsgrove House, Lower Moor Way, Tiverton, Devon EX16 6SS, England; email: katyc@halsgrove.com